Living God's
DREAM
for You

JULIE CLINTON

HARVEST HOUSE PUBLISHERS

EUGENE, OREGON

Cover by Koechel Peterson & Associates, Inc., Minneapolis, Minnesota

Cover photo © Sondra Paulson / iStockphoto

LIVING GOD'S DREAM FOR YOU
Copyright © 2008 by Julie Clinton
Published by Harvest House Publishers
Eugene, Oregon 97402
www.harvesthousepublishers.com

Library of Congress Cataloging-in-Publication Data
    Clinton, Julie, 1961-
    Living God's dream for you / Julie Clinton.
        p. cm.
    ISBN-13: 978-0-7369-2112-1 (pbk.)
    ISBN-10: 0-7369-2112-5
    1. Christian women—Prayers and devotions. I. Title.
    BV4844.C635 2008
    242'.643—dc22

                                                            2008016225

Printed in the United States of America

        08 09 10 11 12 13 14 15 16 / VP-SK / 12 11 10 9 8 7 6 5 4 3 2 1

Foreword

by Karen Kingsbury

Every one of us needs that special time with God, time to draw near to Him and find strength so we can carry on in a way that will bring glory to the Lord and rest to our souls. As an author with a wonderful husband and six children, my life can be busy. I'm sure yours is too. Our weeks are filled with school projects and performances, soccer practices and baseball games, drama schedules and opening nights—all of which will never come again. We're busy for a very good reason. But we can only carry on with our schedules if we make time for God first.

That's where my adventures with Extraordinary Women come in. When Julie Clinton and my friends at Extraordinary Women asked me to be a regular speaker with their national tour, at first I questioned whether it would be one more demand on my time, something that perhaps would put me over the edge. I agreed to do a single event, and I brought my husband along. The outcome was amazing. Don and I had valuable time together—something we don't always easily find—and I was lifted and touched by the power of the Holy Spirit working among the speakers, artists, and thousands of women at the event.

Since then, I look forward to my time at Extraordinary Women events, and I see those weekends as the retreats God intends them to be. I bring my mom and either my husband or one of our kids, and we have special time both in and out of the conference. But here's the reality—every weekend cannot be an Extraordinary Women retreat. Because of that, we need something to help us have that connection with God and the people He has placed in our lives, something that will be a part of our daily walk with Christ. That's where a devotional like Julie Clinton's becomes a priceless tool.

I truly hope to see you at one of the Extraordinary Women events in the coming years. Maybe you were at an event this weekend, and we had the chance to meet each other, to share a few minutes of friendship. But after you've gone home and the soul-stirring music has slowly faded, you'll still have this devotional as a reminder of our time together. In that way, every day truly can be extraordinary.

Visit my website to see when I'll be at an Extraordinary Women event in your area, or to check on my upcoming novels. I am grateful to consider you my friends.

In His light and love,
Karen Kingsbury
www.KarenKingsbury.com

A Note from the Author

Whatever we vividly envision, ardently desire, sincerely believe in, and enthusiastically act upon must inevitably come to pass, provided there is scriptural authority for it.

Dr. William R. Bright

founder, Campus Crusade for Christ

Discovering God's dream...

March 12, 1990. As I lay in the hospital bed, I dreamed about the things we would do together. Shopping, tea parties, sleepovers, Barbie dolls, playing dress up... And someday those days would turn into real manicure and pedicure appointments together, into long talks about God, faith, family, friends, and of course, boys.

I was so thrilled to have had a baby girl that day!

My daughter, Megan, is now 18 years old. And I don't mean to embarrass her, but I'll never forget the days she'd dress up in her finest gown and strut around the house as if everyone in the world was to stop what they were doing and come to the Clintons' just to gaze at her beauty. When she was satisfied that everybody had seen her, she'd look up at me with confidence and say, "Mom, I am going to be a princess when I grow up."

I'd just smile. Then I'd tell her she already was.

As I watched her grow into toddlerhood, I continued to dream. I thought of all the things that she could become and the possibilities that existed for her life. A famous musician, a doctor, a lawyer, a therapist like her dad, a missionary. Megan could do anything she wanted to do. (I still believe that today!)

But now that my baby girl has entered college, our relationship has changed. And as you can imagine, it's been quite a tough adjustment for mom! My role as mother has shifted. No longer am I just a shoulder to cry on for a bruised knee. Now I am a shoulder to cry on for a wounded heart. No longer do I pack her lunch for school or have dinner on the table at night. Now I am just thankful for coffee dates and shopping trips. Though it's tough to say goodbye to my little girl, I am so thankful for our journey together as friends.

Walking alongside her as she pursues God's dream for her life is a real privilege. She taught me a lot about change. And she even allowed me to see that my dreams for her are not necessarily God's dreams. I know that He has a plan for her, and I am so thankful that she desires with all of her heart to live that dream.

I want you to know today that God has a dream for you too! Yes, you. And He wants to reveal that dream to you. But you must earnestly seek Him because simply seeking God is part of His dream for your life. God won't magically appear and tell you His dream for your life (though sometimes I wish He would). Instead, the Bible says that He rewards those who diligently seek Him.

As Megan and I were talking together recently about God's dream for our lives, I realized the need for a devotional to accompany my first book, Extraordinary Women, a book designed to help women in their journey of discovering God's dream for their life. What better way to stay encouraged than to have a daily companion that can direct you to God's Word and what it says about the plans He has for you.

"For I know the plans I have for you," declares the Lord, "plans to prosper you, not to harm you, plans to give you a hope and a future" (Jeremiah 29:11).

God anxiously awaits the day He can align the desires of your heart with His perfect plan. And when you discover God's dream for your life, you begin a new journey that unlocks your greatest potential. This devotional is not "Ten Easy Steps to Finding God's Dream for You." Instead, it's about a journey. A daily journey you are on to growing in your relationship with God and hearing His Word.

Use this devotional as a tool to aid you in reading the Bible. As you do, I believe you will be well on your way to discovering God's dream for your life.

From my heart to yours,
Julie

Living Your Dreams

I came so they can have real and eternal life,
more and better life than they ever dreamed of.
JOHN 10:10 MSG

Ever met a woman who appeared to have it all—nice clothes, successful husband, perfect kids—and yet still lived a seemingly small, unhappy life? It's sad.

You may think that circumstances determine whether you can live out your dreams, but I disagree. I've come to believe there are two kinds of people in the world: those who sit back and resign themselves to the way life is, and those who refuse to give in. The second group chooses to live boldly despite the obstacles they encounter.

Take Joni Eareckson Tada for example. She has learned to live life to the fullest despite a diving accident that left her paralyzed and confined to a wheelchair. The difference is not in the circumstances. The difference is in the attitude. And the only difference between a positive attitude and a negative attitude is the decision to choose one over the other. Extraordinary women choose to hold on to and live their dreams regardless of their circumstances. Jesus came to give you real life. Are you choosing to live it?

Dear Father, help me to live in Your joy every day. Fill my
heart and mind with love and peace and happiness regardless
of what happens in my life. Give me a fresh perspective to
face whatever circumstances surround me. Amen.

The Dream Unfolds

Know that the LORD is God.
It is he who made us, and we are his.
PSALM 100:3

God's dream for you begins to unfold when you start seeing yourself through His eyes. To Him you are extraordinarily special.

Remind yourself daily of what the Bible says about you:

- God made you in His image. You reflect the most wonderful being in the universe (Genesis 1:27).
- You are a child of God (1 John 3:1).
- You were created for God's pleasure (Psalm 149:4; Ephesians 1:4-6).
- You are unique. No one else is like you (Psalm 139:13-14).
- You are given gifts by God that are made just for you (1 Corinthians 12:4-6,11).
- God has placed a calling on your life (Psalm 138:8; Ephesians 2:10).
- God knows everything about you, and He loves you just as you are (Psalm 139:1-3).
- God knows your name. You belong to Him (Isaiah 43:1).
- God loved you first (1 John 4:19).

Each morning when you get up, look in the mirror and say, "I am unique...I am loved...I am God's child." Your identity is firm in His love and in His image. Read these verses and memorize these truths.

Thank you, Lord, for loving me and making me so
special. Help me to see myself in Your image, and
remind me how special I am in Your eyes. Amen.

Receiving God's Love

*God told them, "I've never quit loving you and
never will. Expect love, love, and more love!"*
JEREMIAH 31:3 MSG

God loves you. And because He does, He is chasing after you—yes, *you*! Even now, you might struggle to believe that with so many people and so many problems in the world, God still has time to pursue you—but He does. It's time to let yourself be caught. His love is like no other. Receiving it is a choice. You can begin by praying, *Yes, Lord, I believe.*

Sometimes, your experience with God can mirror the relationship you have with your earthly father. But the two really have no connection. To fully embrace God's love, you must first understand how much God really loves you—regardless of the status of your relationship with your earthly father. You must be available and open to receive God's love, even if you do not fully understand a father's love for you.

Every day, the Creator of the universe, the Most High God, the Giver of Life, pursues you. He longs to love you. Stop running. Let yourself be captured. Let yourself be loved. Let your life begin anew in the everlasting, ever-loving arms of the Father.

*Dear Lord, pour Your love on me. Let me feel Your
loving arms. I don't want to continue running. Thank
You for all You are and for all You do. Amen.*

The Step Master

The steps of a good man are ordered by the LORD, and He delights in his way. Though he fall, he shall not be utterly cast down; for the LORD upholds him with His hand.

PSALM 37:23-24 NKJV

Ah, the StairMaster. Gotta love it! I just step on, punch in my designated time and level of activity on the display, and it starts. I use the guiding pull of the machine, and I climb! My steps are ordered and predetermined. Only one thing is required of me...I must be willing to follow.

Following God, having your steps ordered by the Lord, doesn't guarantee success in every endeavor. In fact, some lessons that God wants to teach can only come through failure. When you fall, however, He doesn't allow you to be "utterly cast down." Instead, He helps you back up so you can learn what He wants to teach you and move on with joy and hope.

The only real failures are those who give up on God, wallow in self-pity, and refuse to get up and go on. As with the StairMaster, if I choose to get off of the path that is laid out for me, my workout is over. I've failed. But if I choose to stay the course, I achieve success.

Choose today to follow the Step Master, the One who delights in you and "upholds you with His right hand."

Dear Lord, I choose to follow You today. I want to walk on the path You have laid for me, even if it means suffering and failure, for I know that You will uphold me. Amen.

The Love of Your Life

*Nevertheless I have this against you, that
you have left your first love.*

REVELATION 2:4 NKJV

Crazy in love. You remember the feeling, don't you? The "I can't get you out of my mind—out of my life" love? You couldn't seem to get enough of each other.

But then something happens. The pressures and demands of the world begin to take hold. Staying close to one another gets more difficult. And as it does, your enthusiasm may begin to wear off. Your attempts at closeness and intimacy can become mechanical and cold.

Our relationship with Christ may be similar. As new believers our love for God is full of passion. We want to walk closely with Him through the day. We think about Him all the time. We long to know more intimately the one who has forgiven us. And we can't help but tell those around us about the love of our life.

But gradually the zeal and passion for God can wear off as the demands and pressures of the world weigh in. That's the time for renewal—for making our relationship with God our top priority.

Spend time with your first love. Make it an everyday priority. As you do, you will find that the fire in your heart for the one who rescued you will be rekindled, and the romance you first knew with Him will be everlasting and ever more fulfilling.

*Dear Lord, rekindle in me that passion for You I once had.
Draw me near so I can find joy in Your presence. Amen.*

A Touch of Hope

Daughter, you took a risk of faith, and now you're healed and whole. Live well, live blessed! Be healed of your plague.

MARK 5:34 MSG

One of the most inspiring stories in the Bible is about a woman who hemorrhaged for 12 years (Mark 5:25-34). Though we don't know her name or her circumstances, we do learn enough to feel sympathy. She is desperate, penniless, and hopeless—until she hears about Jesus. She knew that if she could just get through the crowd and touch Jesus, she would be healed.

With faith and hope as her determination, she managed to reach out to and touch Jesus. A tender touch. Not just the touch of someone jostled in the crowd. It was the touch of a believer. Instantly she was healed. Jesus then speaks to her, "Daughter, your faith has healed you."

Jesus longs to speak the same words to you and me. It doesn't matter where you've been or what you've done. What matters is who He is. He's the hope giver and your answer to a renewed body and mind that are free from the power of sin. He can deliver you from heartache. His dream for you is waiting—just one touch away. Reach out to Him. Touch Him and believe.

O Lord, giver of hope, I want to have faith. I want to have hope again. I want to realize Your dream for my life and live it in hopefulness and joy. I'm reaching out to You, Lord. Touch me. Amen.

The Power of Perspective

*Why has the Lord brought us to this land to fall by the
sword, that our wives and children should become vic-
tims? Would it not be better for us to return to Egypt?*

NUMBERS 14:3 NKJV

Ever met someone who complains about everything? That drives
me crazy!

Chronic complainers gripe about anything and everything. The
Israelites had grumbled against God and Moses since they left Egypt,
and they continued to complain (Numbers 14:1-4). God was fulfilling
the dream He had for their lives, but all they could do was complain.
They just couldn't seem to catch God's perspective of what was going
on in their lives.

In every circumstance, we have a choice: We can complain, or
we can trust God's ability to handle any situation. Complaining
means inaction; faith means moving ahead with God. Perspective is
everything. When feeling hopeless, we should check our perspective,
remembering where God has brought us and allowing Him to work
new miracles in our lives.

What is your perspective today? Have you lost hope in God's
dreams for you? If so, ask Him to change your perspective. "And we
know that all things work together for good to those who love God,
to those who are the called according to His purpose" (Romans 8:28
NKJV).

*Dear Lord, I pray that You will search me and know me this
day. Reveal to me any attitudes or perspectives I may have that
are selfish or that lack faith. Increase my faith today and help
me to change my perspective to align with Yours. Amen.*

Laughing Matters

God has brought me laughter, and everyone
who hears about this will laugh with me.
GENESIS 21:6

My daughter, Megan, and I recently were sitting in the downstairs living area watching TV when suddenly a little hairy mouse scurried out from behind the couch, ran by our feet, and hid behind a plant next to the fireplace! As Megan and I screamed frantically for help, my husband, Tim, came rushing downstairs to the rescue. This was *no* laughing matter. (I think he is more afraid of mice than I am!)

As I watched Tim try to catch the mouse in a Tupperware dish, I didn't know whether to laugh or cry. What was he thinking! Just then, a furry black thing came flying through the air and onto my son, Zach, who jumped about five feet in the air. Tim had grabbed a black pair of socks on the way down the steps to use to scare us as he was catching the mouse!

We were hysterical. It all became a laughing matter!

I believe God laughs with us in moments like these. Laughter is the medicine we all need to help us discover the joy He's placed in our hearts. Regardless of what is going on in your life, you can always laugh with the Lord—turning average situations into laughing moments. The wonderful paradox of faith is the insurmountable joy you can experience when circumstances seem to be at their worst—even if you see a mouse!

Learn to laugh because laughing matters!

(By the way, Tim caught the mouse in the Tupperware bowl!)

Dear Lord, help me learn to laugh, to smile, and to enjoy
life. Open my eyes to the precious moments around me
every day. Thank You for the gift of laughter! Amen.

Dream Dad

Have we not all one Father? Did not one God create us?
MALACHI 2:10

My father passed away several years ago after a long battle with cancer. He died far too young. I still miss him—a lot. But I have many wonderful memories of him. He loved me and really cared for me. He was so kind to me. I know that he helped make me who I am today. That's what made losing him so difficult!

You may have wonderful memories of your father as well. Perhaps he was a great dad who played with you, listened to your jokes, attended your class plays and piano recitals, splurged by letting you buy just the perfect dress for a special occasion, and cheered you up and cheered you on through the variety of moments in your life.

But then again, you may not have such joyful remembrances for a variety of reasons. Regardless of whether you had a father's love here on earth, you have God the Father's love from above.

He is the ultimate Father—your Dream Dad. He is the Father who will always love you when your earthly father ceases to or when his love, as wonderful as it may be, is just not enough to satisfy. God's love is pure, boundless, and perfect. His dream for you is that you willingly open your heart and joyfully accept His endless love.

Your heavenly Father loves you. He wants to embrace you. Curl up in His arms and embrace Him. He longs to be close to you!

Heavenly Father, open my heart to receive Your boundless love.
Help me to realize that Your love is far greater than any father's love
I have experienced here on earth. Draw me near, Lord. Amen.

Everyday Graces

*From the fullness of His grace we have all
received one blessing after another.*

JOHN 1:16

Most of the time when we talk about God's grace, we are referring to the gift of salvation. But God's grace also comes in tiny little packages marked "A Gift for You." Each day God presents gifts of His grace. Most of the time we take them for granted.

Take some time to appreciate some of these gifts:

- freedom to be real
- quiet moments
- walking
- a friend who listens

- a sunrise
- the brilliant colors of spring
- knowing you're loved
- a child's hug

Start looking at each of these as little dreams come true. God's dream for us unfolds in thousands of little ways through everyday graces He places in our lives.

Too often we are just too busy to notice. Or we are so eager to have the big dream come true, we forget to watch for little things that *are* the dream coming true.

Most Christians can trust God for heaven and eternity with Him, but we struggle to trust Him for everyday life. Start seeing and living differently—it will turn your life around!

*Thank You, God, for Your abounding grace, for the
tremendous gift of salvation, and for the thousands of
little graces You send my way each day. Amen.*

The Strength to Do It All

I can do everything through Christ who strengthens me.
PHILIPPIANS 4:13 GOD'S WORD

Dream, beauty, princess... some people hear these words and immediately think *weak, frail, helpless.* I suppose they have read too many fairy tales because it doesn't necessarily have to be that way. Being a princess of the King of kings, as you are, is completely different.

If you believe in God's power, you can do anything through Christ who gives you the strength to handle it. Just think—you have the power to accomplish great things. Even with this power, though, don't try doing it alone. It's not in *your own* power that you can accomplish your tasks and duties. You must rely on Christ's power that is living within you.

We all try to get by on our own. We have the best plans, the greatest intentions. We work hard and long. We worry, sweat, and even panic. Then everything goes wrong, and it all fizzles out.

It's time to realize that you can't do it alone. For true success in anything, you have to be sure that your motives are pure, that the plan you have in mind is from the Lord, and that His power is within. When these ingredients are all lined up, you will be able to accomplish anything and everything!

Too often, Lord, I struggle and strive on my own. Help me to rely on You, to hold on to the strength that comes from You to accomplish everything I do. Amen.

Transformation

Don't copy the behavior and customs of this world, but
let God transform you into a new person by changing
the way you think. Then you will learn to know God's
will for you, which is good and pleasing and perfect.

Romans 12:2 NLT

God's dream for you is a magnificent one. He has great plans to transform you into a brand-new person. There's just one thing—you have to yield to His way.

The first thing you have to do is ask yourself this: *Am I like everybody else in the world? Am I copying the behaviors and customs of the world around me? Or am I different?*

God wants you to be holy because He is holy (Leviticus 11:44). And the only way to be holy is to be different from the rest of the culture and society that swirls around us. Just as royalty is set apart from the masses, as a princess of the King of glory, you must show yourself to be different from all others. You are God's child, who lives to serve Him!

Transformation begins with the mind and what you think about. Let your desire to please God consume your mind, heart, and life. Yield to His will for you, and then your life will be transformed into one that is good, pleasing, and perfect—your dream come true.

O Lord, I give You my life. Transform me into a new person
through Your love. Fill my mind with pleasing thoughts, fill my
heart with perfect love, and fill my life with Your goodness and
glory. Let the world see me transformed into Your holiness. Amen.

A Life of Influence

In everything set them an example by doing what is good.

TITUS 2:7

You will influence other people today. What message will they get from you? Better yet, how will they describe you after today?

Whether we realize it or not, we influence other people's lives. Sometimes we intentionally choose to influence others, but other times we are completely unaware of our impact. The influence of both our good and our bad gestures and words is immeasurable. Perhaps God intended it that way to keep us humble. Often, the people we touch don't realize the effect we had until years later. But what matters most is that we are willing to make every day count by investing in the life of another human being. Make a plan to increase your influence in the lives you can realistically touch. Your investment in other people is the only thing that will outlast you.

You are the hands and feet of Christ, and others are influenced in their own walk with Him by watching you live out yours. To live in a way that lifts up Jesus and honors God is a mighty big calling, but it's something we must do every day.

What message are you sending to the girl behind the counter at the supermarket? To your children? To your coworkers? The question isn't whether you are making a difference. That's a given. The question is, what kind of difference are you making?

Use my life, Lord, as an example of Your love. Use my hands to show kindness. Use my tongue to speak praise. Use my mouth to spread joy and laughter. Let all that I am help others to experience Your love. Amen.

Knowing God Better

*In the morning I lay my requests before
you and wait in expectation*

PSALM 5:3

Our lives fill up quickly with the activities of family, friends, kids, husbands, and households. In our fast-paced world, we often forget that we need time to clear our minds. We need quiet moments to consider concepts larger than *Do I have car pool today? What time does the game start tonight? What will we have for dinner?* Many of us plan to spend more time in devotions and prayer—requiring quiet time to let our minds rest and be still.

In order to know God's leading, you have to turn off the cell phone, the TV, the computer, your iPod or CD player, and anything else that will disturb your calm and quiet. God does not yell. He doesn't use a megaphone or a loudspeaker. He comes in the cool of the day (Genesis 3:8), at dawn (Matthew 28:1; John 8:2), or in the calm of the evening (John 20:19). He speaks in a whisper (1 Kings 19:12).

He speaks to you when your mind is relaxed and you're ready to be tucked in for the night. Or in the moments of the morning before the world awakes. He comes ever so quietly. So be prepared to listen! He has great things to share with you!

*Dear Lord, quiet my busy mind so I can hear You whispering
to me. Let me desire time alone with You each day to share
my thoughts and to hear Your dreams for my life. Amen.*

Surrendering All

Surrender to God!
JAMES 4:7 CEV

Why do we feel safer driving our car than flying when we know that we're more likely to wreck our car than die on a plane? The answer is that we like to be in total control.

We experience this tension every day. We desire control in circumstances because that makes us feel safe. But it's deceptive. Are you really in control driving your car? What about the other people on the road? What about all the moving parts in the engine? Will the brakes work?

The truth is that we have never been in complete control. Believing we are is an illusion we cling to every day. It's easy to believe God and surrender all to Him when we feel as if we're in control, when life is good, when things are going easy. But as soon as we feel as if we've lost control and our circumstances become too much to bear, surrendering and trusting Him gets more difficult. Too often in life God must bring us to a place where we literally have nowhere else to turn but to Him.

Letting go means feeling unsafe, unprotected, and vulnerable. If you're not willing to go there when things are good, God may have to take you there.

He calls us to let go. To open our fists and relax. You'll find that when you give your deepest desires and biggest concerns to God, He surprises you by making a way where none was apparent. Open your fists. Give up control. Surrender all.

I want to surrender all to You, O God, but I am afraid of letting go. Calm my fears and increase my faith so I can willingly hand over my life, my all, to You. Amen.

Setting Priorities

But seek first his kingdom and his righteousness, and
all these things will be given to you as well.

MATTHEW 6:33

What if you were given $86,400 every day for the rest of your life? What would you do with it? Let's add one caveat. You have to spend all of it each day! Could you do it? How would you spend it? Tough decision, right? Guess what—God gives you 86,400 seconds every day, and you spend every one! Every day! How are you using your time?

Most of us are so harried and desperate just to get through another day that we don't take the time to step back and ask ourselves if what we're doing really matters and if our activities reflect our priorities. Often the two are disconnected, though we may be too busy to see it. But the Bible says, "For where your treasure is, there your heart will be also" (Matthew 6:21).

Do the things you do reflect eternal treasures? Are you seeking His kingdom with the time you've been given? What are you pouring your heart into? Take a personal inventory. Find out where you're investing your time and whether the expenditure reflects your priorities. Be sure to spend your time wisely. You never get it back!

Dear Lord, You have given me every minute of the day as a
precious gift. Help me to use my time wisely on the things that
are most important to You and to me. Let me see clearly what
You want me to do with my time, and give me the courage
to say no to those things that just clutter my day. Amen.

To-Do or Not To-Do List

He has showed you, O man, what is good. And what
does the LORD require of you? To act justly and to
love mercy and to walk humbly with your God.

MICAH 6:8

What would we do without lists? They are everywhere! The grocery list, the carpool list, the Target list, the school activities list...we even find lists—of what to do and what not to do—in the Bible! (Exodus 20:3-17).

With every list comes a choice. You can either complete the list or choose not to complete the list. "To act justly and to love mercy and to walk humbly with your God" is God's list of requirements for His children. Three simple yet difficult requirements. Act justly, love mercy, walk humbly...if only it were that easy!

We often forget the first part of that verse. "He has showed you." He has given us an example to live by through His Son, Jesus Christ. Everything that Christ did on this earth was just, full of mercy, and done in complete humility. Choose today to follow His lead, and you will feel a sense of accomplishment when you complete His list for you!

Dear Lord, help me to prioritize my life daily by
completing Your list first. Help me to give each day,
and the tasks laid before me, to You. Amen.

When God Says No

*Going a little farther, he fell with his face to the ground
and prayed, "My Father, if it is possible, may this cup be
taken from me. Yet not as I will, but as you will."*

MATTHEW 26:39

If you're like me, you have times when you feel as if God hasn't come through for you. You pray and pray and—nothing. Or He tells you no! When this happens, we wonder what we're doing wrong.

The good news is that prayer is not about us. It's about finding God's will—God's dream for us. Even Jesus, who was without sin, was given no for an answer. In the garden of Gethsemane, He prayed that the cup of suffering would be taken away. Fortunately for us, the cup was not taken from Him. He went on to die for our sins to redeem the world.

You can be living in the will of God, doing nothing wrong, and still receive no for an answer to prayer. God is pleased with you for submitting your requests to Him even though He may say no. His answer reflects the best course of action for your life. Trust Him, and you'll see why.

*O Heavenly Father, help me to understand Your will
for my life. Help me to know in my heart that Your
will is the very best option for me. Amen.*

The Privilege of Prayer

I have called you friends.

JOHN 15:15

Ever go through a time when you didn't know how to or what to pray for? When Tim and I struggled early in our marriage, I felt speechless at times. Oh, I had words for him! But with God, the words just never seemed to come out. What do we do in moments like that? I've learned through those times to simply dialogue with Jesus about the pain in my life.

Tell Him your hurts—just as you would share with your best girlfriend. Allow Him to speak back to you through words of Scripture, songs of inspiration and encouragement, the words of a dear and wise friend, or the simple impression on your mind and spirit that all will be well because He is in control.

Remember, Jesus calls you His friend, and He prays for you. Isaiah 53 reminds us that He carried our sorrows and is acquainted with grief. I don't know your story, but He does. He knows your pain. He knows your circumstances. He knows your fears. And the Bible says that in these moments, when you don't know how to or what to pray, the Holy Spirit prays for you (Romans 8:26).

Allow Him to shield you in His arms. Allow Him to be your strength and comfort. He is your friend!

*Dear Lord, may I never forget the suffering You
endured for me. Help me to know that You are a friend
who will never leave me. Thank You! Amen.*

Tongue-Tied

*He who guards his lips guards his life, but he
who speaks rashly will come to ruin.*

PROVERBS 13:3

Have you ever experienced foot-in-mouth syndrome? You know, when words are coming out of your mouth faster than your brain is processing them? And before you know it, you're asking for a "do over." It's like asking, "So, when are you due?" to the gal who isn't pregnant. We've all had some moment in time we wish we could do over. We wish we could take back those harsh words that tore at the heart of our husband, saddened our children, or crushed a girlfriend.

The tongue is more powerful than we often realize. James writes, "With the tongue we praise our Lord and Father, and with it we curse men, who have been made in God's likeness. Out of the same mouth come praise and cursing" (James 3:9-10). As extraordinary women, we have a huge responsibility and a great opportunity to use our tongues for good. How have you been using your tongue lately? Have you been using it to build others up or tear them down? Have you been using it to nag, nag, nag or to love unconditionally? As you go throughout your day, remember, "He who guards his lips guards his life"!

*Dear Lord, help me to use my tongue for praise and not cursing.
Help me to go about seeking ways that I can build others up
with the words I say. "Set a guard over my mouth, O LORD;
keep watch over the door of my lips" (Psalm 141:3). Amen.*

Chasing Butterflies

They followed worthless idols and became worthless themselves.
JEREMIAH 2:5

When I was little, I loved to chase butterflies. (My husband, Tim, wishes he had that on video.) Butterflies are beautiful and display an amazing variety of types and colors. But for me, trying to catch them was sometimes like chasing the wind. I didn't catch many.

In life, we often chase after things that don't matter, and they become diversions from what really does matter. Think about it. What are your distractions? Too much TV? Drama in your family or friendships? Other people's agendas? These things consume a lot of emotion and energy, and in the end we realize we played another mindless game that hurt relationships and took away a few more years from our life. Ugh.

Is your life full of distractions? Are you giving your heart, your time, and your resources to things that don't matter? To endless cleaning that doesn't matter, to friendships that aren't going anywhere, to excessive work? It's time for a change!

God's dream is that you would walk circumspectly, redeem your time, and spend it wisely (Ephesians 5:15-16). Invest your time in your relationship with Him and the other significant people in your life.

Chasing butterflies once in a while is fine. Just don't let your husband catch you on video.

God, help me to stop chasing after worthless things
so that I won't become worthless. Instead, help me to
redeem the time by walking in Your ways. Amen.

The Hidden Strength of Pain

*I take limitations in stride, and with good cheer, these
limitations that cut me down to size—abuse, accidents, opposition, bad breaks. I just let Christ take over!
And so the weaker I get, the stronger I become.*

2 Corinthians 12:10 msg

God is not wasting the pain in your life. He never wastes a wound.
He's healing you at this very moment and using that pain to show you
a dream bigger than you realize. But you need to trust Him. When
you trust, you allow room for hope.

When we are in the deep, deep valley, we must hold on to the
assurance that God stands firm and strong behind us. Nothing we
experience will be wasted. It will all be used for our good—to make
us stronger, to make us walk closer to Him, to give us a more loving
heart. In our greatest pain we need to lean heavily on God. He's using
our weakness to do His work in and through us, building trust, so
that His dream for each of our lives can become a reality.

We rarely understand how God is using pain in our lives to refine
us. Sometimes through the tears we can't see anything, much less
understand. But just because we don't understand the pain doesn't
mean He's not using it. He is. It's part of His plan and purpose. Trust
Him.

*Dear God, some days I don't know how I will get through the day
with the pain and hurt I have to face. Let me feel Your presence,
Lord, so I can trust You and relax. Let me fall into Your everlasting
arms, giving You control as I feel Your strength. Amen.*

The Freedom Giver

*Now you are free from the power of sin and have
become slaves of God. Now you do those things that
lead to holiness and result in eternal life.*

Romans 6:22 nlt

Alcoholism, abortion, anorexia, bulimia, depression, infertility, addiction, promiscuity, marital infidelity...problems in life are inevitable. But that's not the main issue. Rather, it's what we do with the problems that separate the extraordinary from the ordinary women of the world. Some people fight through the pain. Others submit to its devastating effects of shame and guilt. Lingering shame from your past will keep you in bondage. Remember, your past is not your past if it's affecting your present.

But Christ wants you free. "It is for freedom that Christ has set us free. Stand firm, then, and do not let yourselves be burdened again by a yoke of slavery" (Galatians 5:1).

God's willingness to redeem pain is infinite. Let Him redeem yours. Your healing may well lead to some of the most meaningful relationships you'll ever enjoy.

Pray for freedom. Pour out your heart to God. Ask Him specifically to release you from the burden you're carrying. And trust that He will be faithful to respond to your request.

*Dear Father, today I present my past to You—all the sins and pain
I have lugged around for years. Redeem them for Your good and
Your glory, and give me freedom to live as a new woman. Amen.*

Reach Out

Rejoice with those who rejoice; mourn with those who mourn.
ROMANS 12:15

Parties are so much fun! Celebrations bring so much joy! (Unless, of course, you are the one planning it all!) I recently planned a surprise birthday party for my daughter, Megan, that took weeks of preparation and scheduling. The hardest part was trying to keep it all a secret! I thought I would never be finished in time! Luckily, Megan's best friend and some of our friends and family reached out and took care of some last-minute details. Because of their help, the party was a huge surprise and success! We all rejoiced in the precious gift Megan is to us, and now we have a memory to last a lifetime.

But it was in a much different way that some of those friends reached out to our family several years ago. My father, at the age of 59, was diagnosed with multiple myeloma—bone marrow cancer. He was in a fight for his life. We prayed fervently for healing, but God saw fit to take him home to heaven. We grieved. Encouraging words, visits, cards, e-mails, and prayer all comforted us as friends reached out and mourned with us. Their willingness to reach out and be used by God helped us become strong as a family today and able to support others as they now go through this same crisis.

Reach out to someone today, rejoice with them, mourn with them, and see the goodness of God come alive through you!

Dear Lord, help me to learn to see others the way You see them. Help me to rejoice with those who are rejoicing in life and to be there for those who are in mourning. Give me the discernment I need to notice the feelings of others. Amen.

Anger Management 101

Get rid of all bitterness, rage and anger, brawling and slander, along with every form of malice.

Ephesians 4:31

Okay, don't stop reading because of the title. Anger is not always the easiest topic to discuss, I know, but it's real. Anger is an emotional reaction associated with other negative feelings like hurt and sadness. My husband, Tim, has often taught that anger is an outpouring of what's inside the heart—a God-given emotion in response to a real or perceived wrongdoing or injustice in life.

Paul stresses in his letter to the church at Ephesus that in order to be pure vessels used by God, we must deal with anger.

Hurt is usually at the core of anger. God's dream for you is to be free of the hurt and anger that enslaves you. That doesn't mean you don't feel it, it means you don't sin in it and allow it to hold you in bondage. Hurt that is not dealt with leads to anger, and anger leads to resentment and even bitterness. Are you hurting today? Who or what has hurt you? Are you tired of feeling angry? It's time to work through the anger, to let it go, and to let God heal your heart.

Dear Lord, help me to let go of any hurt, anger, or bitterness in my heart and give You control. I want to be like You in true righteousness and holiness. Amen.

The Foundation of Life

The rain came down, the streams rose, and the winds
blew and beat against that house; yet it did not fall,
because it had its foundation on the rock.

MATTHEW 7:25

Daniel is an intelligent man. He worked his way quickly up the corporate ladder, married Kristyn, and had two great kids. With everything going for him, he was set for life.

Bryan, on the other hand, struggled to make a living. He and Elise married at a young age, had three children, and struggled to put food on the table. Then, suddenly, their middle son died of an illness. Medical bills piled up. The pain did too.

Two families at two extremes. Which would you rather be? The story goes on. The difference in these two families lies not in finances, life circumstances, or social status. Instead, it lies in where they placed their security. Daniel's social standing and financial status were not enough to keep his marriage together. Long trips away from home and tension when he came back dissolved his marriage.

Bryan and Elise were different. They placed their security in Jesus Christ. The men at the factory took up a collection to pay for medical bills. Even the church pitched in. The community support surrounding the family was a testimony to their foundation.

What is your foundation? Where is your security placed? God's dream for you is to have Jesus Christ, your Rock and Redeemer, as the solid foundation you need to build a strong and healthy life—an abundant life, filled with joy and purpose!

O Lord, when the storms of life rage around me, help me to
cling to You, my Rock. With You as my strong foundation, I
can be sure that my life will be firm and secure. Amen.

The Daily Grind

*May the LORD repay you for what you have done. May
you be richly rewarded by the LORD, the God of Israel,
under whose wings you have come to take refuge.*

RUTH 2:12

A coffee shop not far from our office is called the Daily Grind.
Not a bad name for a coffee place. But it's usually the name we give
to everyday life. Cranking out the daily grind includes doing the
dishes, laundry, going to work, bathing the kids, making your husband happy, feeding the dogs, taking them out, and dealing with a
million other issues in your life every day.

If you're like me, you probably wonder if people really understand
all that you have to do. If they did, they'd probably help out a little
more. That's the old daily grind.

Sometimes I wonder if anybody really sees what I do and knows
what my life is like. But God does. He sees the things we think go
unnoticed every day. That's why He says to do everything as to the
Lord, for there is a reward (Colossians 3:23). Your faithfulness will pay
off. And your attitude as you do these things every day will determine
whether you will enjoy the ride.

One day He will reward you for being a wonderful, virtuous, godly
woman. Start counting your blessings, and you'll see.

*Thank You, Lord, for seeing me even when I don't feel as
if anybody else does. I pray You would meet with me in the
mundane so I can approach every day with exceeding joy and
without growing weary. I pray in Jesus' name. Amen.*

That I May Fear Your Name

Teach me your way, O LORD; and I will walk in your truth;
give me an undivided heart, that I may fear your name.

PSALM 86:11

Ever have difficulty trying to decide where to go for dinner? Imagine your parents are in town and want you to go with them, but your husband must attend a banquet and has invited you to join him. Your heart is divided between two loves.

Such distractions are often minor. But major ones exist too. You fight internal battles every day—battles with your thought life, envy, temptation, and so much more.

The way to battle distraction and fleeting pleasures is to fill our minds with the truth of God's Word.

Jesus taught us that we cannot serve two masters. Our hearts cannot share the pleasures of this world with the pleasures of God. We must choose this day whom we will serve. Has your heart been divided? Have you lost sight of the purpose for which you were created? If so, may your heart connect to the plea of the psalmist so you can follow the way of the Lord.

Dear Lord, shield me from the temptations of the world that bombard me every day in a thousand ways. Help me to focus on You and Your purpose for my life. With my eyes focused on You, my heart will stay undivided, loyal only to You. Amen.

Is It Nap Time Yet?

*He will not let your foot slip—he who watches over you
will not slumber; indeed, he who watches over Israel
will neither slumber nor sleep. The LORD watches over
you—the LORD is your shade at your right hand.*

PSALM 121:3-5

When Tim and I brought home our firstborn, Megan, we were so happy—and exhausted! She had colic and hardly slept. One night, Tim was staying up with her, but he could hardly see straight. I heard her fussing and went in to check on them. He was out, stone cold! She was talking and cooing. Tim and I had a little chat about that.

But imagine a God who constantly watches over us and sees what is happening in our lives. According to today's verse, that's who He is—a God who cares about what happens to us, to you, 24/7. He's there for us, and He's in complete control.

God's dream for you is to find rest in Him. Trust that He knows what He is doing. Believe that He will take care of you—always!

*Dear Lord, it is so comforting to know that You are in
control all of the time. Thank You for watching out for
me and for Your unending protection. You are amazing!
Help me to rest in Your arms all day long! Amen.*

I Have Decided

Choose for yourselves this day whom you will serve.
JOSHUA 24:15

Decisions, decisions, decisions…every day is full of them. It starts as soon as we wake up. What will we wear? What will we make for breakfast, lunch, and dinner? What will we watch on television (then again, who gets time to sit down long enough for TV)? What chores will we do first…and the list goes on and on.

I believe that a full life is lived in the moment of a decision. For instance, when driving, you can decide whether to turn right or left to get to your destination. And in that moment, you either journey closer to where you want to go or you move farther away. In a more personal example, if a mother decides not to allow the rebellion of her children to dictate her self-worth and effectiveness as a mother, she chooses to take a step toward the full and abundant life God has for her. In John 10:10, the Bible says, "The thief comes only to steal and kill and destroy; I have come that they may have life, and have it to the full." A full life is God's dream for us fulfilled in different ways for each individual.

When you decide to hold on to and live your dreams regardless of your circumstances, you're on your way to living in God's dream for you. Today, take a moment to think about each decision as a path to the full life God desires and dreams for you!

Dear heavenly Father, guide me in Your will for my life. Help me to seek Your face first and foremost before making any decision on my own. I know that apart from You, I can do nothing. Help me to stay on Your path for my life! I love You, Lord! Amen.

How to Slay a Giant

A champion named Goliath, who was from
Gath, came out of the Philistine camp.

1 SAMUEL 17:4

What discourages you? What keeps you from being all that you can be? Think about that for a moment. Now ask yourself, *Have I made agreements with my discouragements? Have I given up, listened to their lies, and allowed them to ruin my joy and defeat me?*

Most describe Goliath as a man of huge stature. More than nine feet tall—that's a giant! But in life, giants come in all shapes and sizes. They can even come with names—self, money, work, loss, relationships...you get the picture. And usually they threaten us, discourage us, and immobilize us.

So how do you slay a giant? I love what Max Lucado said: "Two types of thoughts continually vie for your attention. One proclaims God's strengths; the other lists your failures."*

Don't run from your giants. Face them. You've got to believe that God is greater and will strengthen your heart. Find God's strength. And over time He will give you what you need to overcome. Five small, smooth stones—just when you need them.

Dear Lord, I want to give You the giants in my life right now. I am tired of focusing on my failures and discouragements, and I want to depend on Your strengths. I believe You are fighting for and beside me. Give me the stones I need to slay the giants in my life. Amen.

---

* Max Lucado, *Facing Your Giants: A David and Goliath Story for Everyday People* (Nashville, TN: Thomas Nelson, 2006), p. 106.

The Heavenly Bride

*Hallelujah! For our Lord God Almighty reigns. Let us rejoice
and be glad and give him glory! For the wedding of the
Lamb has come, and his bride has made herself ready.*

REVELATION 19:6-7

Weddings are more popular than ever, and the wedding industry is booming. Have you ever seen the movie *Father of the Bride*?

Men often think women are silly to want a large, lavish wedding with all the trimmings and fanfare. But in spite of what guys may think, weddings are wonderful and glorious things. The book of Revelation talks about the future relationship of God and His church in wedding terms. Revelation describes "the wedding of the Lamb," where the bride is clothed in "fine linen, bright and clean."

The apostle John's vision of the future is filled with wedding images that delight all of us—light and bright, white and shining, robes of splendor, thrones and kingdoms. The Holy City, the new Jerusalem, is described "as a bride beautifully dressed for her husband" (Revelation 21:2). Now this is the kind of thing we women can relate to!

And we all should be able to relate to how magnificent the future will be—more than anything you could ever dream of yourself. These magnificent visions described by John are not just fairy tales or imaginative dreams. They are true promises of what is to come. They depict your real future when Christ comes in glory and God unviels a new heaven and a new earth. This is God's ultimate dream for you—to live in glory with Him forever and ever.

*Almighty God, thank You for these visions of the future kingdom.
Help me to live my life in constant gratitude for Your gift of
salvation and the hope of being with You in glory. Amen.*

Living in Peace

*I am leaving you with a gift—peace of mind and
heart. And the peace I give is a gift the world
cannot give. So don't be troubled or afraid.*

JOHN 14:27 NLT

"Just give me some peace and quiet!" Ever scream that at the world?
I have.

Our world never seems to be at peace. Wars are raging, and we hear
the grim statistics every day on the news. It seems that almost weekly we
hear about a shooting at a school, in a mall, or in a neighborhood.

Throughout world history, peace has eluded mankind. And you
can expect it to stay that way until Christ comes again. In the mean-
time, how are we supposed to live when conflict rages around the
world? Strife is across the street, across town, across the sea. What can
we do to bring peace into the world?

Accept God's gift of peace He has offered to you. "Don't worry
about anything; instead, pray about everything. Tell God what you
need, and thank him for all he has done. Then you will experience
God's peace, which exceeds anything we can understand. His peace
will guard your hearts and minds as you live in Christ Jesus" (Philippians 4:6-7 NLT).

You won't find peace in this world. You'll find it in your heart as
you lean on the Lord and stay close to Him.

*O Lord and Father, I know that there will not be complete peace on
earth until You come again. While I wait for that great day, I pray
You will open my mind, my heart, and my life and fill it with Your
peace—a peace that exceeds anything I can comprehend. Amen.*

Priceless Detours

*Enter by the narrow gate. For the gate is wide and the
way is easy that leads to destruction, and those who enter
by it are many. For the gate is narrow and the way is
hard that leads to life, and those who find it are few.*

MATTHEW 7:13-14 ESV

Detours are inevitable. As I look back on my own life, I see God's hand in each and every one—the difficulties Tim and I had early in our marriage, Zach's hospital stays as a little boy, my father's death.

Discovering God's dream for your life is a matter of accepting that your life is not your own. Few, if any, lessons are learned when the path is easy. The windy road with the potholes and the detour signs will challenge the heart. But the emotional and spiritual growth is priceless.

If you want to discover God's dream for your life, you must come to the end of yourself. For "whoever finds his life will lose it, and whoever loses his life for my sake will find it" (Matthew 10:39).

When life gets difficult, surrender your plans to God. The detours will lead you to the end of yourself and to the true beginning of your intimacy with Him.

*Dear God and Father, forgive my impatience when life takes turns
and detours I'm not fond of. Change my perspective that I may
see Your hand in the sudden stops and the altered directions I'm
not expecting. Let me stay calm as I follow Your plans. Amen.*

Never Alone

You know Him, for He dwells with you and will be in you.
JOHN 14:17

Pagers, cell phones, the Internet, instant messaging, text messages...technologically we are closer together than ever, yet relationally we couldn't be further apart. Loneliness is one of the great social ills of our day.

Our world is full of lonely people. A life void of the Holy Spirit is a vase without flowers. It's empty. The prophet Jeremiah compared God's people to jars of clay (Lamentations 4:2), but with God as our Potter, we can be molded, shaped, and filled with the Holy Spirit. In John 14:17, Jesus promises the Spirit will live with us...and *in* us.

Friend, you're never alone. Even when your dreams are broken, you can trust God's Word. Store it in your heart today because the way will get rough; the slope will get slippery. When it does, you can trust that the Holy Spirit is *in* you...helping you remember His promises and driving away despair's darkness with the light of divine comfort.

God made you as a vase to be filled with the Spirit's beautiful bouquet of love, joy, peace, patience, kindness, goodness, faithfulness, gentleness, and self-control.

It's an aroma pleasing to God...the very fragrance of Christ.

Let Your Spirit fill my life with joy, O Lord, so my despair and loneliness will vanish. Let my heart overflow with the light of Your love and the gifts that only Your Spirit can give. Amen.

Your Influence Matters

As I was with Moses—so I will be with you.

JOSHUA 1:5

"God's calling in your life never lacks God's supply."

I heard that line when I was in college but really didn't understand it then. Years later, after a little more life experience, I have come to believe it. We are here, like Jesus, to be about our Father's business. To do the will of Him who called us.

Whether you realize it or not, you have a position of influence and a call for your life. You may not lead the Israelites through the desert for 40 years, but you do have influence in the lives of those around you. You help your kids with their schoolwork and encourage them in sports. Maybe one of your parents has fallen ill, and you're called to their care. You may be the emotional support your husband needs as he struggles to survive the corporate world, or the glue that holds together the women's ministry at your church. As a woman of God, your calling could be to help others through their wilderness.

God's words to Joshua—"Be strong and courageous"—echo to us today. As God calls Joshua into the wilderness, look at what He tells him to do. Joshua is to ground himself in the law (Joshua 1:8). If you want the map for your life, you've got to read the Bible. Be bold in what you believe God wants you do to. Be strong and courageous.

Ponder the Word. Practice the Word. Then, the Bible says, you'll be prosperous as you lead others through the wilderness.

Help me, Lord, to be strong and courageous so I can influence those You have asked me to lead. Amen.

A Peaceful Mind

*You will keep in perfect peace him whose mind
is steadfast, because he trusts in you.*

ISAIAH 26:3

"When I find him, I'm going to give him a piece of my mind!"

"I've got a mind to..."

"I think I'm losing my mind!"

I imagine you have heard or maybe even used one or more of these statements before. Or consider the United Negro College Fund campaign slogan: "A mind is a terrible thing to waste."

With all that we have going on in our lives, focusing our mind on any one thing is often difficult. As women, we must multitask at all times in order to get anything accomplished. "Losing our mind" becomes a common daily occurrence!

So how do you keep your mind steadfast and find peace? I believe it begins by having a personal quiet time with God each day. You must make time to have a relationship with Him. I am not talking about hours at a time, although it's great if you have that kind of time. What I am referring to is the quality of time you spend with God, not the quantity. During your time with Him, He will focus your mind; He will sustain you and keep you in perfect peace! Make time for Him—every day!

*Dear Lord, help me to remember to make time for You
daily. Help me to have a steadfast mind that is focused
on the dream You have for me today! Amen.*

Created for Relationships

Let us make man in our image.
GENESIS 1:26

You don't have to go very far in the Bible to realize that we are made for relationships with God and with significant others in our lives. In fact, Genesis 1:26 is the first reference in the Bible showing the Trinitarian nature of God Himself: "Let *us* make man in *our* image." We serve a relational God. Three distinct persons—the Father, Son, and Holy Spirit. One God.

The Scripture is clear—we were not made to be alone (Genesis 2:18). Yet so much today is ripping and tearing at our relationships and challenging our love and affection for our husbands, our children, our friends, and our coworkers. Our time with God is an increasingly precious commodity.

Created *not* to be alone—so many lay in bed at night crying themselves to sleep, just wishing somebody would understand them. They long for someone to know them, just to be with them. But God doesn't want that for you. His dream is for you to be in vibrant, healthy, edifying, fruitful, refreshing, encouraging relationships. To know He is there for and with you.

Ask yourself today, *What challenges are keeping me from an intimate relationship with my Creator, God? What is affecting the relationships with those I love?"*

Don't let aloneness trump the joy of healthy relationships in your life.

Father, thank You for making me in Your image. Reveal the barriers holding me back from seeking You and help me to develop intimacy with You. Please give me the courage to face the things affecting my relationships with those I love the most. Amen.

Opportunity over Obstacle

The land we passed through and explored is exceedingly good.
NUMBERS 14:7

The glass is half full or half empty. It all depends on how you see it. Everything we do or don't do hinges on the way you view life. Consider the scouting report brought back to Moses from the promised land (Numbers 13:26-33). Ten spies said, "No way." To them the area was a horrible place, full of fierce giants and fortresses. Too tough to tame! They focused on obstacles.

Joshua and Caleb had a different perspective. They saw an exceedingly good land, flowing with milk and honey. Opportunity. In a way, both reports were true. The difference was perspective—faith versus fear. Opportunity over obstacle.

Only God clearly sees the big picture—the dream in all its glory. "Now we see but a poor reflection as in a mirror; then we shall see face to face" (1 Corinthians 13:12). What's the view where you are? A glimpse of faith's rainbow in a troubled sky? Or dark, churning clouds hovering on the horizon?

Sometimes, what we see depends on what we're looking for.

Dear Lord, help me to see clearly what dreams You have for my life. Change my perspective on the world into one of hope that I may see Your glory and Your vision. Amen.

Choosing Freedom

*Now the Lord is the Spirit, and where the
Spirit of the Lord is, there is freedom.*

2 CORINTHIANS 3:17

Attitude. It's everything. It's the one thing you have complete control over. How you respond to your circumstances—positively or negatively—is your choice. But it's not easy.

The path to freedom begins when you realize you always have a choice—even when you feel you don't. In the darkest times of life, when your options seem limited, you still have a choice. You may be required to choose between bad and worse. You may be able to choose between good and great. But the choice is yours. As long as you are willing to exercise the freedom of choice, you will always have the opportunity to get better, be better, and do better in life.

Our heavenly Father sent His only Son to die for you so that you can experience true freedom. He showed His love in a way that you cannot ignore. Freedom includes choosing to embrace what Jesus did on the cross on your behalf and allowing your life to be different as a result. You must be willing to think differently once you've accepted that grace. No longer do you depend on your own strength and abilities.

God's dream is that you would live in His freedom, not in fear. The choice is yours. Choose to walk in Him, fulfilling His desire for your life!

*Dear Lord, show me the path of true freedom. Help me to yield
to You and embrace Your life-changing gift of grace. Amen.*

A Little Bit of Morning

*But I cry to you for help, O LORD; in the morn-
ing my prayer comes before you.*

PSALM 88:13

Reading this passage of Scripture, I am reminded of a story behind a beautiful song by Christian music artists Phillips, Craig, and Dean that I heard them tell at a concert. One member's young daughter was always eager to rise out of bed. Extremely early one morning, she ran into her father's bedroom, woke him up, and said, "Hurry, Daddy, there's a little bit of morning outside! Time to get up!" How precious is the mind of a child.

Think about it…God's mercy is available to you, brand-new, at the beginning of every day. And He wants to meet with you! His love never fails. He wants to listen to your prayers and meet with you in the morning. Early. Every day.

Are you feeling distant from God? Do you need more of Him? We all do. Beloved sister, God knows what you are feeling. Claim His promise of love, wipe away the tears, and wake up to meet with Him in the little bit of morning outside. You'll be glad you did!

*Dear Lord, I am so thankful to know that Your love and mercy is
available at the dawn of every new day. Help me to rest assured that
Your compassion will never fail me and that Your faithfulness to me is
greater than I can ever imagine. Because of You, I have hope! Amen.*

A Constant in Times of Change

*Every good and perfect gift is from above, coming
down from the Father of the heavenly lights, who
does not change like shifting shadows.*

JAMES 1:17

Our daughter, Megan, just graduated from high school. And our
son, Zach, is quickly becoming a young man. Watching your kids
grow up and prepare to move out can sure be tough.

Solomon reminds us that life continues to march on, even through
a series of inevitable transitions. He mentions times for birth, death,
weeping, laughing, mourning, dancing, silence, speaking, war, and
peace (Ecclesiastes 3:1-8). Do any of those sound familiar to you?

As joyous or painful as they may be, these shifts are natural parts
of life, and best of all, they can be filled with meaning! If you have
God in your life, you can trust Him through the changes, knowing
that every day brings you closer to your eternal destiny in the presence
of God Himself. Solomon even pointed out that God set eternity in
your heart (Ecclesiastes 3:11).

Take every opportunity you can to find eternal significance and
meaning in the changes and transitions you experience. Change is *not*
the only constant. God Himself is an unchanging God, the Alpha and
Omega, the beginning and the end. Take comfort in that. He will
always be there and ready to sustain you!

*Dear Lord, I want to make You first in my life—in every thought,
every decision, every move. Draw me closer to You so I can achieve
this goal. Let me hear Your voice so I can know Your will and
walk in it through every change and transition in life. Amen.*

Pilates, Mirrors, and God

Do not merely listen to the word, and so
deceive yourselves. Do what it says.

JAMES 1:22

Most of us have sat in front of the television with a pint of Ben &
Jerry's while watching a "little" (don't you just love them?) workout
video. Later, as we pass by the mirror, we wonder why we don't look
like those trim women we just spent 45 minutes with. What happened? I know I heard everything they said. It was the legs kick I
struggled with.

When you walk past the mirror of your own walk with God,
are you shocked? Do you want to hide? Reading, listening to, and
knowing God's Word are important in your faith walk, but they are
meaningless if you don't obey the Word or apply it. The effectiveness
of our Bible study and the Sunday sermon is measured by our behavior
and attitudes throughout the entire week.

Live the Word every day. It will change your life! Don't give in to
the temptation to listen to wise words without applying them to your
life. Be a living testimony of God's grace and truth. His dream for
you is to make His Word come alive in your life daily!

Father, help me to be a doer of the Word and not just a hearer.
May I be so infected by Your words of truth that my actions are
reflections of what is deeply engraved on my heart. Amen.

Seeing You Through

The LORD said, "I have indeed seen the misery of my people in Egypt. I have heard them crying out because of their slave drivers, and I am concerned about their suffering."

EXODUS 3:7

One of my favorite passages is in the Old Testament book of Exodus. God loves Israel the same way He loves each and every one of us. And when Israel was suffering pain and affliction, when they felt as if everything was going wrong, He saw them. And He didn't just see them. The Word says He was committed to coming down and loving them. And He did.

If you move from the early books of the Bible to Revelation, you'll always find God in the midst. I don't know what you're going through today, but I know God does. I don't know what challenges are ahead for you, but God does. And I believe He will deliver you. He will give you strength and everything else you need not only to survive, but to thrive.

Come to Him with a spirit of expectation, with confidence that He will see you through.

Father, thank You for always understanding how I feel and being there for me. Give me a spirit of expectation, an assurance that You will see me through. Amen.

Broken Dreams

Consider it pure joy...whenever you face trials
of many kinds, because you know that the test-
ing of your faith develops perseverance.

James 1:2-3

Has your heart ever been crushed or your dreams shattered? If you are like most women, you answered yes. The loss of a boyfriend in high school. The loss of a job. Even the loss of a loved one. Broken dreams and grief are parts of living in this fallen world. Christ reminds us that in this life we will have suffering and times of trial that will often seem too hard to bear.

Take heart. God said in His Word that He will *never* forsake you or abandon you in times of heartache. He will be your strength in times of weakness. "Though you have made me see troubles, many and bitter, you will restore my life again; from the depths of the earth you will again bring me up" (Psalm 71:20). "For just as the sufferings of Christ flow over into our lives, so also through Christ our comfort overflows" (2 Corinthians 1:5).

What a relief! Be encouraged with God's love for you today. Lean on the Dream Giver and trust Him to restore you with His comfort and peace.

Dear heavenly Father, help me to see that You are the mender of my
soul and my comfort in times of pain and sorrow. Help me to lean on
You today in the midst of any storm that may cross my path. Be my
strength when I am weary, and help me to trust You fully. Amen.

The Perfect Outfit

Man looks at the outward appearance,
but the LORD looks at the heart.

1 SAMUEL 16:7

With a glittering tiara, yards of pink toile, and a layered full-length skirt, an ordinary girl is transformed into a dream princess. What we wear can certainly change our attitude about ourselves. Dress us up, and we feel and act like a princess. Throw on the old jeans and a ratty T-shirt, and we feel like Cinderella scrubbing the hearth. A part of us knows we get treated like royalty when we look the part.

But God sees far beyond the perfect outfit you're wearing. He looks at how you clothe your heart. In Paul's letter to the Colossians, he says to clothe yourself with compassion, kindness, humility, gentleness, patience, and love. This type of clothing is far more important than keeping up a princess appearance. Nice clothes can certainly help you feel good about yourself, but the clothing on the inside, the virtues that are referred to in the Bible, are of greater importance. How you dress on the inside—the way you treat your family, your husband, your friends, and any other person you interact with throughout your day—is what really matters.

Dress yourself from the inside out. That will make all the difference in the way you approach the world. Staying in style on the outside is fine, but be sure that you have an attitude full of the Spirit of God on the inside. Don't just talk the part, dress the part.

Search my heart, Lord, and fill me with Your Spirit. Clothe me with
righteousness and love so everything I do will glorify You. Amen.

Growing in the Lord

*Grow in the grace and knowledge of our Lord and Savior
Jesus Christ. To him be glory both now and forever! Amen.*
2 PETER 3:18

We are told to grow in the grace and knowledge of Jesus Christ and
that if we keep our lives focused on those two things, we will continually walk close to God our Savior. But maybe you're like me, and
you're wondering, *How do I do that?*

Growing in God's grace means you appreciate and enjoy living in
His favor. You are constantly surrounded by His blessings and His
boundless goodness. You must understand and appreciate these gifts.
And above all, you have been given the gift of salvation.

Growing in the knowledge of Jesus Christ includes continually
coming to know Him better by reading the Word, talking to Him
in prayer and seeking and yielding to His plan for you. As you grow
in Him you will become like Him, living for the sake of others (not
yourself) and acting in kindness and compassion.

The ending to Peter's letter is a blessing and prayer for you. May
it truly become part of your life. After all, you are who you spend
time with!

*Dear Lord, show me the way to live and grow in Your grace. Increase
my knowledge of You and of Your Son. Make me yearn for a life
lived with a focus on You. I pray all of this in Christ's name. Amen.*

Growing Up

God wants us to grow up, to know the whole truth
and tell it in love—like Christ in everything.

EPHESIANS 4:15 MSG

As a teen, I couldn't wait to grow up and go to college. Growing up seems like such an easy thing to do when you're young. Ask some children, and they'll tell you they want to get big, to grow up, to be older.

However, as we grow into adulthood, we find that growing and changing can sometimes create uncertainty and hurt. To take on a new job assignment can be challenging. To move away from everything that is familiar, to start a family, to face an empty nest...changes like these are rarely easy.

Often during these life changes we need to rediscover ourselves and our abilities to handle new and different responsibilities. Practice these tips for handling it all:

- Go with God. Don't try living life without Him. He will never leave you or forsake you, regardless of what happens (Deuteronomy 31:8).

- Make a plan. Break down the latest challenge into steps rather than trying to tackle the whole thing at once.

- Get enough sleep. Change can be exhausting, so allow yourself the time you need to rest.

- Keep something that's familiar—a routine, a comfy bathrobe, dear friends (even if now they are long distance), or favorite foods.

Lord, help me to handle the challenges of growing up and changing.
Be near me and guide me into Your great plan for my life. Amen.

A Future Hope

*I have it all planned out—plans to take care of you, not
abandon you, plans to give you the future you hope for.*
JEREMIAH 29:11 MSG

God has a plan for your life. Yes, your life and mine. The tragedy is
that we're often too busy—too preoccupied to hear Him or see His
work in our lives.

If you slow down and begin to "see" Him and spend more time
with Him, you'll see how God gently takes you by the hand and leads
you, a little at a time, to the future that only He can see. By moving
you along gently, He gives you the time you need to mature, to develop
the skills you need for the work He has planned, and to get used to
the idea that all that's happened in the past may in fact be part of His
grand plan for you.

By revealing His plan a little at a time, God helps us adjust to the
idea that His dream may be bigger than we ever imagined.

*O Lord, I trust that Your plan for my life is perfect for
me. Reveal to me, even in small ways, how You are
fulfilling what You have dreamed for my life. Amen.*

A Great Coach

And I will teach you the way that is good and right.

1 Samuel 12:23

Both of our children love playing sports. If you played sports growing up, you probably can remember some good coaches and some bad ones. We all know the impact a coach can make—either for good or for bad.

When I read about the life of Samuel, I often think of him as a great coach. His responsibility was to make sure the people followed the way of the Lord. Read 1 Samuel 12:20-24 today and look at his coaching skills. He said, "I will pray for you." His outcome was specific: to know God and make Him known.

I don't know about your kids, but mine, left to themselves, could easily get lost and confused along the way. What about your husband? Or better yet, what about you? Left to ourselves, we get wayward quickly. Who is speaking into your life right now? Do you have a godly mentor? An older and wiser woman, a Titus 2 woman who can speak truth and encouragement into your life? If you don't, ask God today to bring someone you can trust, someone who can coach you as you follow the way every day.

*Father, I pray today You would use me as a great coach
to lead others into the way of the Lord. Help me to find a
wiser woman to mentor and pray for me as well. Thank
You for using others to build us up in You. Amen.*

God Is All You Need

My grace is enough; it's all you need. My strength
comes into its own in your weakness.

2 CORINTHIANS 12:9 MSG

Ever try to divide your time and attention evenly and fairly among family, friends, deadlines, expectations, work demands, and church obligations? Life can get difficult fast. But you can manage it by understanding this one principle: *God is enough.* Once you understand it and apply it to your life, you can suddenly move from the mundane to the unimaginable and from the uncertain to the certain.

When things are falling apart around you, God is enough. When illness invades your life or that of a loved one, God is enough. When you feel you've lost your way, God is enough. When life is out of control, God is enough.

Focusing on God's sufficiency is the most important step toward experiencing God's dream for you. Remember, the journey isn't about capturing the dream; the journey is about knowing the God who placed the dream in you to begin with. If you focus on the dream and not God, your focus is misplaced, and you'll get lost and stumble. But if you focus on God first, He will provide what you need to grasp the dream.

Know that God loves you and that He is enough to see you through. God has always been changing the world, one woman at a time.

Help me to realize, Lord, that Your grace is all I need
regardless of what happens in my life. Stand close to me
and let me feel Your presence so I can be set apart from the
world and shine Your light on all around me. Amen.

A Fairy-Tale Transformation

*If anyone is in Christ, he is a new creation; old things
have passed away; behold, all things have become new.*

2 Corinthians 5:17 nkjv

A tarnished past becomes a shining future. Nightmares are turned into beautiful hope-filled dreams. Maids are transformed into Cinderellas. Ugly ducklings into swans. A frog into a prince.

These are childhood fairy tales, but transformations aren't impossible! With Christ, transformation is not just a dream; it can be a reality—for you!

The Christian life is a progression. We don't just suddenly do better, act better, and make wiser decisions. But with God we can change. Neither is everything all rosy and sweet in the Christian life. In fact, sometimes things tend to get even harder. But as we invite Christ into our lives, learn about His nature, and grow in Him, we begin to change. The more we know about Him and the more we experience His presence and unfailing love for us, the more we are able to move boldly and confidently into the world, believing that with God all things really are possible.

But God requires you to cooperate. Transformation begins with your response to Him. Remember, you are a work in progress. Instead of waiting on God, consider that God may be waiting on you. His dream for you is being fulfilled every day. But He wants you to respond. Ask Him today to show you the way!

*Dear Lord, transform me into the person You want
me to be—perfect and holy. Help me to see Your
vision for me as You sanctify my life. Amen.*

A Way to Lighten the Load

Moses' father-in-law replied, "What you are doing is not good.
You and these people who come to you will only wear yourselves
out. The work is too heavy for you; you cannot handle it alone."

EXODUS 18:17-18

Admit it—as a society we're overloaded and stressed-out most of the time. The pace and pressure of our day pile up and affect our physical, emotional, and mental health. They distort our attitudes at work, at home, and even in our ministries. Pushed to the limit, we become exhausted and ultimately ineffective.

But God doesn't expect us to do everything alone. Even Moses was advised by Jethro, his father-in-law, to ask for help and delegate some of the work. Asking for help is not a sign of weakness—in fact, it shows character.

I don't know what you're wrestling with, but I do know that right now, somewhere in your life, some people are just waiting for you to ask them to help you. God has them there for you. Maybe a friend can give you a break from caregiving responsibilities. Or a supervisor will assure that your work gets done as you go through chemotherapy. Or a credit counselor is waiting to help you get back to financial freedom.

Only you know what's weighing you down. But Jesus stands ready to help you figure out how to lighten the load, and He has placed people in your life to assist you. All you have to do is ask.

I often make the mistake, Lord, of thinking I should handle
everything myself. Open my eyes to the willing hearts and open hands
around me. Help me to have the courage to ask for help with things
that are overwhelming my life and my heart right now. Amen.

Dream Record

Write down these words...

EXODUS 34:26

When you were a young girl, did you ever dream of making your own record or becoming some other kind of celebrity superstar? I think we all have. The TV show *American Idol* has become phenomenally popular as viewers watch everyday people (some of them a little *too* everyday!) compete for a recording contract that will lead them to stardom.

You can make your own kind of dream record—not a CD, but a personal record of the God-given dreams He has laid on your heart. Who knows what this record will lead to in your own life?

It has often been said that in order to make something a reality in your life, you must write it down. The Bible has made the importance of writing clear—from the recording of the Ten Commandments to the instruction the Lord gave to Moses in Exodus 34:27, "Write down these words, for in accordance with these words I have made a covenant with you and with Israel." In Deuteronomy 27:3, the Lord instructs Moses, "Write...all the words of this law when you have crossed over to enter the land the LORD your God is giving you."

If you haven't already started a "dream record," let me encourage you to start one today! You will be amazed at how much of a blessing this record will be in your life for generations to come.

Dear heavenly Father, thank You for having a dream just for me. As I record this dream, help me never to forget that You are sovereign and that You have a plan for my life. May future generations be blessed by the great work You have done. Amen.

A Glimmer of Hope

*Find rest, O my soul, in God alone; my hope comes
from him. He alone is my rock and my salvation; he is my fortress, I will not be shaken.*

PSALM 62:5-6

What's the purpose of lighthouses? I know this—they're beautiful.
Pictures of them adorn many homes.

But for sailors, that light at the top of a cliff overlooking the stormy
sea is a ray of guidance—a glimmer of hope that they will safely dock
their vessels.

What about you? Do you need hope today? I know this—God is
close to those who are brokenhearted. He knows what you are going
through. And better yet, He's there with you in the midst of it all.

I know of a breast cancer survivor who began lacing up her shoes
to run a race, determined to raise awareness of this horrible disease.
Though it's a race she never thought she would live to run, she now
offers hope to those struggling with the same pain. She chose to be
the vessel God wanted to use to offer a glimmer of hope to women
who feel as if they have none.

If you're in need of hope today, look around. God is in the midst.
And if you see someone in need, be open—God wants to use you!

*Dear Lord, God of all hope, thank You that I can trust
in You. Regardless of my circumstance, I know You are
all I need. Help me to place my hope in You! Amen.*

A Glorious Joy

The LORD your God is with you, he is mighty to save.
He will take great delight in you, he will quiet you
with his love, he will rejoice over you with singing.

ZEPHANIAH 3:17

When do you experience joy? Are your times of joy most intense when you are enjoying good health, in times of prosperity, when all is well?

Maybe it was on your wedding day, Christmas morning, or your child's first day of school. For most, these are days and seasons when we experience joy. Everything seems right.

But can we experience joy in a deeper way when times are tough? Can we know a more profound joy in times of adversity? I think so. Why? Because our God takes delight in us in the mountains and valleys! Understanding this reality is important for your spiritual journey. Finding joy and peace in the low times can only happen with the right perspective.

God's dream for you includes the assurance of a glorious future for the people of God (Zephaniah 3:14-20). You need to put your soul in His hands. Delight in knowing that He cherishes and cares for you. You bring Him great joy!

Dear Lord, thank You for Your loving care. I rest secure,
knowing that You rejoice over me with gladness and singing.
My heart is quieted by Your glorious love. Amen.

A Holy Pursuit

Pursue peace with all people, and holiness, with-
out which no one will see the Lord.

HEBREWS 12:14 NKJV

As women, we want to be pursued. To be desired, cherished, adored, and loved. We want to enjoy meaningful relationships.

However, relationships can be rather challenging. And, we may have unrealistic expectations that are hard to fill. Still, though relationships are often messy, they are worth all the effort we put into them.

Isn't it interesting that the writer of Hebrews associates our relationship with God to our relationship with other people? The depth of our relationship with the Lord will directly reflect the depth of our relationship with others.

Once you begin to pursue God, you recognize what He desires—peace and holiness. And in this pursuit we come to find our lives reflecting His heart.

As women, the desire to be pursued will never change. God created you that way. But you can also turn that desire around so that you pursue Him!

O Lord, fill my heart with the desire to pursue You, to know You
better, and to delight in Your presence. Unite my spirit with Yours
so that I may know Your heart as You know mine. Amen.

A Mother's Love

May the Lord make your love increase and overflow.

1 Thessalonians 3:12

Did you play house when you were little? Ever play the role of mom? For many women, God has allowed that wonderful dream to come true. Living out that dream requires a lot of love. A mother's love is a reflection of the love God gives to His children, and we mothers need to be shining examples of that magnificent love.

Unending, strong, secure, and steadfast. That's a mother's love. It miraculously restores itself after a night up with a child who is thrashing with screams that could wake the neighbors. It is patient through teething and potty training. It endures several trips to the mall in one week to find just the right outfit. It remains steadfast through tears over a rebellious teenager. A mother's love protects from evil by providing children with a rich Christian faith. Her love trusts that the world will be a better place because she has touched a life. It always hopes for the very best. It prays without ceasing.

Thankfully, you don't have to handle this alone. God's love fills you, and with His help you can shower your children with love. You can be an effective mother with the help of a loving God who gives you strength.

*Dear Lord and Father, fill me with Your love so I can have
a ready supply with which to shower my children. Give me
patience and let me find joy in being a mother. Amen.*

A Praying Savior

*It is Christ who died, and furthermore is also risen, who is even
at the right hand of God, who also makes intercession for us.*

Romans 8:34 NKJV

Has praying ever been difficult for you? Many times we get caught
up in the here and now. Our prayer, like a small kite with a big tail,
just won't fly. We wonder, *Why pray when He knows my mind is somewhere else?*

You've got a friend who is praying for you. It's Jesus! He's doing it
right now! He *lives* to make intercession for us (Hebrews 7:25).

Think about that for moment.

As a mom, you live for your kids. As a wife, you live for your
husband. Now, multiply that love and devotion a billion times. As a
Savior, standing at God's right hand (Romans 8:34), Jesus is totally
absorbed in praying for *you*! Just picture Him whispering in the
Father's ear, "She's had a tough day. Let's help her out."

When you can't find the words or strength to pray, remember
there's always one thing to say—help!

If that's as far as you get on a tough day, Jesus understands. And
rest assured that He will take it from there!

*O loving Jesus, hear my cry for help. Let me rest in the thought
that You hear my cry even if it is merely one word, even if it is a
distress call from my heart that I cannot even form into words.
Quiet my heart in knowing You are in heaven, presenting my
every need to the Father. In Your name I pray. Amen.*

A Willing Heart

*Trust in the LORD with all your heart and lean not on
your own understanding; in all your ways acknowledge him, and he will make your paths straight.*

PROVERBS 3:5-6

As we watch others soar through life seemingly unfazed by troubles
and sorrows, we may begin to think, *God may have had a dream for
me too, but I missed it.* Or *I'm too far along in life for God to be able to
use me now.* Or *God might want to use me, but my life is just way too
messed up right now.*

Regardless of your circumstances, your background, your finances,
or your skills, God is looking for a willing heart. With a willing heart
you will be open to God working through you and in you. Circumstances don't matter. The condition of your heart does. Is it open? Is
it ready? Is it available?

A willing heart is something you can develop. The Word says that
when you draw near to God, He will draw near to you (James 4:8).
God is ready and waiting whenever you are. Trust Him through everything you are going through. The secret to living God's dream for you
includes having a willing heart!

*Open my heart, Lord. Make it willing to yield to You and to the
wonderful plans You have for my life. I am trusting that You
have dreams for me far beyond what I have in mind. Amen.*

Abundance Thinking

Who of you by worrying can add a single hour to his life?
MATTHEW 6:27

How do you see it? When times are tough, do you believe there isn't enough to go around? Or are you more prone to trust that there's plenty? Most of us are a combination of the two. Sometimes we believe there is enough to go around, and sometimes we fear there isn't.

Often, when we consider what matters most to us, we fall into what's called *scarcity thinking*. We fear we'll miss out on the job we've been working toward for years or the man we've been searching for. This fear clouds our thinking and leads us to make poor choices.

Abundance thinking, on the other hand, helps us keep life in balance. Instead of thinking, *If not now, when?* you think, *If not now, later.* Instead of thinking, *If I pass on this opportunity, it may never come again,* you think, *If the opportunity doesn't come again, it wasn't meant to be.*

God's dream for you is not just about believing *in* Him, it's also about believing *Him*—that He will provide whatever you need to get through whatever you must.

O Lord, help me to follow Your leading. Let me see through the eyes of willingness and abundance thinking. Help me not to be restless or anxious, but to rest in Your will. Amen.

An Uncertain Destination

*I consider my life worth nothing to me, if only I may finish
the race and complete the task the Lord Jesus has given
me—the task of testifying to the gospel of God's grace.*

ACTS 20:24

Wouldn't it be nice to own a GPS that could somehow help us navigate through all of life's difficult decisions? Detouring around all of the pain and misery would be especially nice. I sometimes wonder what I would do if I knew what really did await me. Would I run and embrace it? Or would I run in the opposite direction?

Without a doubt, the uncertainty of the future can be really scary at times. The apostle Paul faced a lot of uncertainties and often didn't know every detail of his future. But he understood the miracle of living in the moment. Though he did not know the path the Lord would lead him down, he realized that wherever that path led, he had but one task and one responsibility to live out: to believe that God's grace would be sufficient.

You may be struggling with not knowing what the future holds. Instead of focusing on the what ifs, God's dream for you is to focus on what you have been given. Focus on where you are. Embrace the privilege you have to testify to the gospel of God's grace now. As you do, He will reveal your personal destination and give you strength for the journey.

*Lord and Father, help me embrace the here and now, the
moments I am living in, rather than yearn for or fear the future.
Guide my steps and let me rejoice in each path You lead me
down as you reveal Your ultimate dream for my life. Amen.*

An Unchanging Love

Jesus Christ is the same yesterday and today and forever.
HEBREWS 13:8

Unemployment, illness, loss, relocation...in the midst of life's most difficult changes, you can find comfort by knowing that one thing never changes: God's love for you. He's with you in every circumstance, every life change, every situation. In fact, He's not just *with* you—He's *in* you.

Isn't that a relief? God loves you, period. You don't have to earn His love. You don't have to be worthy of it. And nothing you do or have done will keep God from loving you. What a relief to know that your failings won't keep you from the love of Christ. Nothing you can do will change His feelings for you. That's grace!

He is a God of love. His love never changes. His blessings for you abound. His favor endures from one generation to the next. His dreams for you continue to shine and hold fast through every change of your life.

Dear Lord, hold fast to me through the inevitable changes of life, both good and bad. Let me rest secure in the knowledge that Your love for me, my family, and my friends will endure forever. Amen.

Are You Listening?

Be quick to listen, slow to speak and slow to become angry.
JAMES 1:19

Communication involves both sending and receiving messages. Of these two, truly listening to the message you're receiving may be the most important.

Are you listening? Are you paying close attention as you read this? Listening is an essential part of building meaningful relationships. The more we listen, the quicker we see potential pain and miscommunication before they become problems. Yet listening over all the distractions of life is quite a challenge. To truly minister to others, to be a good friend, you must listen. "This is the confidence we have in approaching God: that if we ask anything according to his will, he hears us" (1 John 5:14). When others come to us for guidance, we should guarantee them the confidence that we hear them as God does.

Other people aren't the only ones we need to listen to. Above all, God's dream for you is to listen to Him, to long for His voice in your heart. When you hear it, you become more sensitive to the needs of those around you. And you become more confident in making decisions that will provide support to those in need.

Be a good listener, a slow reactor, and a true friend!

Please open the eyes of my heart, Lord, so I can clearly hear You.
Please open my ears, that I may truly hear those around me. Amen.

Around the Table

Blessed is the man who will eat at the
feast in the kingdom of God.

Luke 14:15

Some of my fondest memories have been made around our dinner table. Discussing basketball with our son, listening to the drama of our daughter's high school class, smiling with my husband...these are the moments I cherish. And of course, we love to eat good food.

Have you ever wondered what God's dinner table looks like? Think about it. I imagine beautiful urns filled with the best flowers. Heaping bowls of the most ripe and delicious fruit ever seen. Serving dishes overflowing with any kind of food you want. The most exquisite china pattern ever designed on each and every plate! To know there is a space reserved just for me is simply breathtaking!

A parable found in Luke 14 speaks of a man who went to great lengths to prepare a dinner banquet for all of his friends. When the dinner was ready, he requested that his servant go and bring his friends to the table to eat. Devastated and angry when the servant returned with no one, this man invited anyone his servant could find—people who were poor, lonely, or homeless—to come and sit at his table to eat. "I tell you, not one of those men who were invited will get a taste of my banquet" (Luke 14:24).

God's banquet table is open to anyone who will believe, but many do not accept the invitation. Do you have a place at His table? If so, thank Him today for reserving you a seat. It will be a dinner you will not want to miss!

Dear Lord, thank You for reserving a place for me
at Your table! Help me to pass along Your invitation
to those I meet who don't know You. Amen.

Awe and Wonder

Therefore stand in awe of God.

ECCLESIASTES 5:7

When singing during worship time at church, have you ever felt as if you were performing for a lip sync contest? Mouthing the words and reciting the prayers with no sense of awe and wonder? Following along without a feeling of adoration toward an Almighty God, without a desire to lift a hand in thanksgiving to the one and only true God, who is worthy of all praise?

When we lose the attitude of awe and wonder, complacency sets in. We begin thinking about everything we have to do and the places we need to go. All of a sudden, the song is over and we have missed an opportunity to praise our amazing God.

Work on practicing the discipline of gratitude. Sit down with your family each night and pray together, simply praising and thanking God. An attitude of gratitude will surely expand your heart into adoration and wonder of the living God, who makes your heart His dwelling place. There is always something to thank Him for. Your eyes will be opened, and your passion will be renewed. Your heart will begin to refocus on what really matters—giving honor and praise to Him who is worthy of all adoration.

Dear Father God, fill my heart and life with gratitude for all You have given me. Increase my awareness of Your great and almighty power. Fill me with the wonder and awe of You. Amen.

Awestruck

Therefore, since we are receiving a kingdom that cannot be shaken, let us be thankful, and so worship God acceptably with reverence and awe.

HEBREWS 12:28

When I was a little girl, I was awestruck with David Cassidy. If you're my age, you remember *The Partridge Family*. Along with every other girl, I thought I was going to marry him. Then I met Tim.

As little girls, we were all in awe of someone or something—good or bad. I am sure you have someone in mind even now. But God doesn't want us to admire "worthless things" (Psalm 119:37); He wants our attention on Him. He wants us to fear Him and to keep ourselves from idols (1 John 5:21). He wants us to "fix our eyes not on what is seen, but on what is unseen. For what is seen is temporary, but what is unseen is eternal" (2 Corinthians 4:18).

Do you need a renewed sense of God's majesty? Are you lacking in wonder over the Lord of the creation? Then it's time to turn your eyes from the idols of the world because "those who cling to worthless idols forfeit the grace that could be theirs" (Jonah 2:8). Take a moment today to soak in the beautiful countryside, or the millions of stars in the midnight sky, or the snow-covered mountains, or the deep, blue ocean, and become awestruck by our King.

Father, soften my heart and open my eyes to Your majesty. Help me to fear You and see You in everything. Amen.

Breaking the Busyness Spiral

Mary...sat at the Lord's feet listening to what he said. But Martha was distracted by all the preparations that had to be made...The Lord answered, "You are worried and upset about many things, but only one thing is needed. Mary has chosen what is better."

LUKE 10:39-42

My daughter, Megan, and I were shopping on the second floor of a large mall recently when all of sudden out of nowhere a police officer went flying by on a Segway PT—you know, the motorized scooter-like machine with two wheels. Obviously chasing a suspected shoplifter, the police officer screamed, "Stop!"

Stunned at what I had just seen, I realized a similar thing takes place in my own life. Sometimes I feel as though God is chasing me, just like that police officer, yet I continue to sprint away from Him.

Take a minute and stop—right where you are. Ask yourself, Have I made time for God today? Or have I been unavailable?

God loves us and listens to us and is never too busy or unavailable. Yet often we're too busy and unavailable for Him. But when we run from spending time with Him, our lives become imbalanced. When this happens, we can spiral downward.

Instead of becoming too busy for God, we need to turn to Him to find balance in life, to steady our heart and slow the pace. If you wait to find time for God, you'll crash. Instead, make time for Him. Get out your daily planner or calendar, and make an appointment with God—today!

You know how busy I can get, Lord. Forgive me for relying on my own power and neglecting time to talk to You. In my busyness, help me to remember to lean on You, for in Your arms I will find strength to accomplish all that is required of me. Amen.

Building with Legos

You see, at just the right time, when we were still
powerless, Christ died for the ungodly.

ROMANS 5:6

Have you ever been so distracted by what *you* wanted that you failed to recognize the strengths, abilities, and help you have through Jesus Christ?

A friend of mine was a nanny for a disabled child for several years. She told me about a particular phase in which the boy constantly wanted to put together Legos. Due to his lack of motor skills, however, assembling even the simplest structure was extremely difficult for him. He became overwhelmingly frustrated, but he wanted to do it alone. It broke her heart to see him cry. He didn't understand that all he needed to do was ask, and she could help him put the pieces together.

As I reflect on this child's frustration when building with Legos, I cannot help but think of the numerous times in my own life in which I have completely failed to accept God's help in piecing things together. Admit when you need help. At the right time, God will offer it. He will provide—just ask!

Almighty God, so often I struggle to do things on my own
rather than calling out to You for Your help. Forgive me.
Help my confidence in You to grow so I will readily call
out to You for Your loving, helping hand. Amen.

Call to Order

For God is not a God of disorder but of peace.
1 Corinthians 14:33

The task of keeping things in order never seems to be done. We have laundry to fold, kids to carpool, bathrooms to clean, dinner to make… and the list goes on and on. Twenty-four hours in the day just isn't enough sometimes! I am often amazed when reminded that God created the entire earth in just one week. What a task that had to be!

It can also be very frustrating when things get out of order in our lives. You make dinner plans, and your spouse calls home to say he will be late, your kids forget to remind you about the game that night, or your boss at work moves a deadline up from two weeks to two days. The result: a life of disorder!

How comforting to know that God is a God of order. When things don't make sense, He does! I love that about God. He is in perfect control of our lives! He desires to remove that feeling of disorder and replace it with total peace—peace that passes all understanding (Phillippians 4:7). Embrace the disorder of the day, smile, and trust Him!

Dear Lord, I am so thankful that when my life is out of order, You are in complete control. Help me to trust You in the middle of my chaos and embrace Your peace! Amen.

Cheerios in a Bag

The beloved of the LORD shall dwell in safety by Him.
DEUTERONOMY 33:12 NKJV

Have you ever been in a hurry and given Cheerios in a bag to your children for breakfast? Or wished that someone had given you Cheerios in a bag for breakfast because it's now two o'clock in the afternoon and your tummy is starting to make loud gurgling noises?

Sometimes life comes at you so fast it seems as if it exceeds the speed of light and will never slow down. As women who are seeking to live out our God-given dreams on a daily basis, we need to grant ourselves permission to take a break sometimes and just breathe. Take a moment and rest in the promise the Lord gave to Benjamin. "The beloved of the LORD shall dwell in safety by Him, who shelters him all the day long; and he shall dwell (or rest) between His shoulders" (Deuteronomy 33:12 NKJV). In verse 27, the Lord says, "The eternal God is your refuge, and underneath are the everlasting arms."

Take a mental picture of God's arms wrapped around you as His daughter and soak in the warmth of His love. My prayer is that you will find rest from the "Cheerios in a bag" kind of day!

Dear Lord, I am so glad that I can find rest in You. Thank You for being my daily place of rest and comfort. Help me to slow down, be still, and know that you are my precious God. Amen.

Open the Door

Look at me. I stand at the door. I knock. If you hear me call and open the door, I'll come right in and sit down to supper with you.

REVELATION 3:20 MSG

How many women do you know who are really free? My hunch is not many. Bondage is everywhere. We're haunted by our pasts, burdened by self-pity, unwilling or unable to forgive ourselves or others, and held captive by our need to control. Instead of living big lives, we live small ones. Instead of living boldly, we live timidly. Instead of running freely, we limp along, dragging the leg irons we've clamped on our own legs.

That's not what Jesus wants for us.

A life with Christ is a life of possibility, of change, and of new beginnings. It's a life of hope and second chances and dreams come true. It's a life of freedom—but only if you choose to embrace the liberty He offers. He wants to come into your heart to set you free.

Being free begins by letting Christ into your heart. He's knocking. Do you hear Him? Open the door and let Him in.

I choose freedom, Lord. Free me from my past, my burdens, my aching heart. Restore me so I can live freely and enormously and abundantly in You! Amen.

Choose Life

*This day I call heaven and earth as witnesses against you
that I have set before you life and death, blessings and curses.
Now choose life, so that you and your children may live
and that you may love the LORD your God, listen to his
voice, and hold fast to him. For the LORD is your life.*

DEUTERONOMY 30:19-20

Childbirth is a miraculous thing. Even with all the pain! When we're born, God breathes life into our body. But along the way, our sinful nature takes root, and we must be saved. As you choose to surrender your heart and your soul to Him, He breathes His Spirit into you, and that's when real life begins.

No life exists on earth or anywhere else in the universe, without the power of God. He is the only one who can give life and take it away. When you decide to choose life, you align yourself with God's dream for you. You cooperate with His will and live for His purpose. You become completely His. There is no better place than at the feet of Jesus.

Who are you living for? Your spouse? Your kids? Your boss? Where are your priorities placed? It's okay to serve those you love. You just need to make sure that in serving those you love, you serve the One who placed them in your life. Choose Christ, listen to His voice, hold on to Him—and live!

*Dear Lord, thank You for life. Thank You for my
family and friends. Help me to embrace the life You
have given me and to live for Your glory. Amen.*

Circumstantial Joy

Yet I will rejoice in the LORD, I will be joyful in God my Savior.
HABAKKUK 3:18

Are you currently going through a difficult time in your life? We cry to God, asking how long must we endure the pain, how long we must wait to feel relief. When we are hurting, joy seems like a foreign concept, an ideal to be reached.

Habakkuk experienced joy in the midst of a difficult time in his own personal life as well as the lives of the Judean people. Having envisioned the devastation and despair of the Judeans as a result of the Babylonian invasion, Habakkuk trembled in fear. He was scared! Yet as he describes what he envisioned for the Judeans he speaks of the joy he feels in the Lord (Habakkuk 3:17-19).

His prayer was not based on his circumstance. Regardless of whether God delivered the Judeans, Habakkuk would always rejoice in the Lord! The wonderful paradox of faith is the amazing joy we can experience when circumstances seem to be at their worst. Just as Habakkuk decided to surrender his fears to the Lord and wait, you too can place your confidence and faith in the God of your salvation regardless of the circumstance.

Dear Lord, help me to wait on You. Give me joy
regardless of my circumstances. I rejoice in knowing
You will be with me always! Amen.

Claiming God's Love

*This is love: not that we loved God, but that he loved us
and sent his Son as an atoning sacrifice for our sins.*

1 JOHN 4:10

Living in such a confusing world, we can easily miss how beautiful
we are to God and how much He really does love us. Learn to long
for the love of God. His love for you is unconditional and free. It
comes as a gift from the ultimate giver of all gifts. All you need to do
is open your heart and say, "Yes, Lord." Those simple words will help
you yield to God's love.

But the evil one hates the fact that you are loved. All hell is trying
to get you to believe God doesn't care about you or doesn't love you.
Your enemy wants you to believe that you mean nothing to God. But
the truth is that God created you, chose you, and loves you with a love
that will last forever (Jeremiah 31:3).

Fight off your fears and claim God's love. Reach out, open your
heart, and ask Him to tangibly show you His love for you. Let Him
fill you with His endless and abounding love. Resting secure in God's
love is an essential element of handling whatever comes your way.

*Dear Lord and Father, help me to stand firm against the evil
one, who tries to make me doubt Your love. Dispel any fears and
doubts that creep into my life, and fill me with Your love. Amen.*

Closing the Gap

The LORD's unfailing love surrounds the man who trusts in him.

PSALM 32:10

Recently, my husband, Tim, was telling me about a car chase he watched on TV. A woman driving close to 100 miles per hour on a California highway was running from the police in a stolen vehicle. "It was wild," he said, "the police were focused on her and stayed with her the entire way…I was on the edge of my seat, watching the whole time to see what would happen next."

This scenario made me think. God never stops chasing us—pursuing us! He created us for relationship and intimacy. And just as Tim watched that car chase from the edge of his seat, God wants us to feel excited and on the edge about Him.

But most of us don't even realize He's pursuing intimacy with us. Or if we do, we may be afraid of it. Many women live with this paradox—desiring intimacy with God but not being sure how to be in such a relationship. Busyness, too much work, and the inability to unplug from our electronic society often get in the way and suffocate the burning flame in our hearts. We may believe Jesus for salvation, but we often fail to believe He can meet the needs of our everyday lives. Where we don't trust, we don't experience intimacy.

Only when you close this gap of unbelief and realize that without Him you can do nothing (John 15:5) do you open the door to true intimacy and begin a love affair with the lover of your soul. Only then will the fire in your heart be glowing anew.

Make a response to God. Draw closer to Him. Your pursuer is waiting.

O Lord, pursuer of my soul, my heart desires to have a close relationship with You. Draw me near to You. Enfold me with Your love. Let my faith increase so that I may know You and love You better. Amen.

Companionship First

Be still, and know that I am God.

Psalm 46:10

Contrary to what you may believe, God is not necessarily sitting at a desk in heaven, calculating how much you get done in a day. He desires your companionship even more than your accomplishments.

But we can easily fall into a performance trap, believing the more we do, the more we matter. The number of things we get done in a day becomes the measure of our self-worth. When we don't get our list accomplished, we feel like failures. We become irritable, we feel unworthy, and eventually we grow even more irritated. Like cancer, our attitude can begin to seep into our relationships with those we love.

As you come to recognize that there's more to life than just your to-do lists, you begin paying careful attention to the needs of those around you—to be understood, affirmed, validated, and appreciated. With the world screaming for you to do more, God gently whispers, "Be still, and know that I am God." He longs to be in a relationship with you, and He rejoices to see you in relationship with others—sharing His love and grace.

Don't get so caught up with the tasks at hand that you miss the opportunity to disciple or minister to somebody who needs your help. Remember, companionship should come before accomplishment.

*Gracious Lord, help me to put my relationships with
You and others at the top of my list, even when the world
demands I accomplish more in a day. Soften my heart so
I will listen and be attentive to those I love. Amen.*

Thankful for the Thorn

To keep me from being conceited...there was
given to me a thorn in my flesh.

2 Corinthians 12:7

Throughout the New Testament, Paul challenged, reprimanded, and encouraged fellow believers to develop a closer, more intimate relationship with Jesus Christ and not to give up when facing the persecution that was so prevalent in the early church. He has become a spiritual giant to me, seeming to be unaffected, if not fueled, by the attempts of his enemies to make him lose his faith in God.

Whatever Paul's thorn in the flesh was, it affected him strongly enough to prompt him to plead with the Lord three different times to take it away from him. The Lord denied this request, however, and promised that His grace and strength would be enough for Paul in the midst of his suffering. How did Paul respond? He did not pout, throw a fit, or begin doubting God's sovereignty or innate goodness. Instead, he accepted God's answer!

Paul did not just accept his infirmity—he became glad for it. He saw the bigger picture. Being released from his challenge would have made life more comfortable and less painful. However, not being released from it gave opportunity for God's grace and strength to rest on him in the midst of his suffering.

Whatever the case, large or small, we all have issues and circumstances in our lives that need the sufficiency of God's grace and strength. Will you choose to respond as Paul did? I hope so!

Dear Lord, help me to rely on Your strength in my time
of weakness. May I learn to see how my struggles can be
demonstrations of Your power in my life. Amen.

Decontamination

The city dump. Leftovers that never got eaten. The diaper pail. What comes to your mind? Stinky. Dirty. Rotten. Contaminated!

Have you ever thought about what contaminates the body and spirit? Drug abuse, alcoholism, secondhand smoke, chemical ingestion...these all contaminate the body. Things that can contaminate the spirit may include the television programs we watch, the books or magazines we read, the songs we listen to, the Internet sites we view. Please understand, I don't mean that every television program, magazine, song, or site on the Internet is contaminated. What I do want you to recognize is this: What we put in is what comes out. Just as bad food sickens the body, so bad media sickens the soul. Scripture commands us to "purify ourselves from everything that contaminates the body and spirit" (2 Corinthians 7:1).

How do you purify yourself? First, you must have a relationship with Christ. You must accept Him as your Lord and Savior. Then choose to grow in your relationship with God. Make time to study His Word regularly and pray. Finally, you must confess your sin and repent, turning away from temptations that would draw you further from God.

God's dream is for you to purify yourself from the things that contaminate your mind, body, and spirit. A woman with a pure heart is beautiful, rare, and extraordinary!

Dear Lord, bring to my attention anything in my life that
is contaminating my body and spirit. I desire to have a
pure heart because I revere You and Your holiness. Cleanse
me today and make me clean before You. Amen!

Designer Fragrance

Thanks be to God, who always leads us in triumphal procession in Christ and through us spreads everywhere the fragrance of the knowledge of him. For we are to God the aroma of Christ among those who are being saved and those who are perishing.

2 Corinthians 2:14-15

Of the five senses God created in us, the sense of smell is one of the best! The smell of a rose. A fresh apple pie just pulled from the oven. Fresh cut grass in spring.

I love this passage in 2 Corinthians because it reminds me that we are the fragrance of God in the lives of others. The Message puts it this way: "In Christ, God leads us from place to place in one perpetual victory parade. Through us, he brings knowledge of Christ. Everywhere we go, people breathe in the exquisite fragrance. Because of Christ, we give off a sweet scent rising to God, which is recognized by those on the way of salvation—an aroma redolent with life."

Because of Jesus Christ, you are a pleasant scent to those you meet! You spread that aroma through your warm smile, gentle spirit, and your kind heart. Take a moment today to smell a sweet scent, to be reminded of God's dream for you, and to allow someone else to smell the fragrance of your life.

Dear Lord, thank You so much for the sense of smell. It's a joy to know that because of Christ in my life, I give off a pleasant aroma to those around me. Shine through me today and bring others to the knowledge of You through my life. Amen.

You've Got Mail

Your word is a lamp to my feet and a light for my path.
PSALM 119:105

I dread getting junk mail and spam. But I love getting important messages and heartfelt notes. If I were to tell you about mail that could literally change your life, would you open it?

The Bible is your special letter from God. It has a living, breathing message that will ignite your heart for life. But opening the Word takes work. To me, the Bible sometimes seems like the heaviest book on the shelf. That's because Satan is hard at work making sure we forget to read God's love letter to us.

Your mind-set has everything to do with whether or not you're reading the Word. Are you approaching the Bible with an attitude of drudgery? Or do you see it as an adventure you can't wait to be a part of? We should come to God and His Word with a spirit of expectation, knowing we are going to encounter the living God!

First, God sent Jesus. Then He sent you a love letter in the form of the Bible. The more familiar you are with Him and His Word, the more intimate the two of you will become.

Open it. Read it. Memorize it. Pray over it. Embrace it. Go to your "inbox" and listen to what God is saying. You've got mail every day!

Thank You, Lord, for sending a love letter to me in the Bible.
Give me a willing and eager heart that yearns for closeness to You.
Reveal Yourself to me as I read Your Word each day. Amen.

Do It Heartily

*Whatever you do, work at it with all your heart, as
working for the Lord, not for men, since you know
that you will receive an inheritance from the Lord as
a reward. It is the Lord Christ you are serving.*

COLOSSIANS 3:23-24

Ever wish you had a rechargeable battery that would alert you when your motivation is low? Wouldn't that be nice? Never again would you have to worry about complacency or apathy setting in to destroy God's plan for your life!

It's so easy to become complacent and to feel stuck in the day-to-day routine of life. I believe the evil one enjoys watching us feel apathetic and inactive. His goal is to get us to feel that way. Many women accomplish their daily tasks without any encouragement, acknowledgment, or words of thanks. Maybe you do too. The daily grind can wear down our enthusiasm, our ferver and zeal.

I'm glad the Lord understands our struggle with apathy. In His Word He encourages us to continue in the work He has for each of us. Someday we'll understand God's purpose for us and receive the inheritance He has waiting for us in heaven! When you don't feel like helping someone, do it anyway. When you don't feel like reading the Bible, do it anyway. Choose to serve Him! You'll be glad you did!

*Dear Lord, help me to guard my heart from apathy and
complacent living. Give me the strength to remain steadfast in
what You have called me to do. Help me to know that what
I am doing is for Your glory and not for men. Amen.*

Do It Right the First Time

The eyes of the LORD are on the righteous.

PSALM 34:15

Sometimes my kids make me crazy. But I think that's probably because sometimes I make them crazy too. There just is so much to do, and we only have so much time to get it all done. Sometimes I push our family too hard to get all our work done.

Did you know that children face an average of about 1200 commands a day? And some moms expect them to respond correctly every time. When they don't, everyone in the family is affected. Bad moods spread like a virus.

But even the best kids accomplish only about 80 percent of the commands they face. And when my kids don't listen to me, I get frustrated because I think my plan is what's best for them. Sometimes, though, I find out it really wasn't the best thing for them or even all that important.

God's not like that with you. His plans are righteous and perfect. And He has given you a manual of life for a reason. When you follow the precepts of God, His blessing can rest on your life. He never pushes too hard, and even when He has to prod us, His steadfast love remains strong. He is always encouraging and challenging us in the way we should go.

Father, life is tough, and I often fall short of living according to Your commands. Please help me to live righteously, to do things right the first time. I pray this in Jesus' name. Amen.

Do Not Be Deceived

All Scripture is God-breathed and is useful for teaching, rebuk-
ing, correcting and training in righteousness, so that the man [or
woman] of God may be thoroughly equipped for every good work.

2 TIMOTHY 3:16-17

Lies. They are all around us—in magazines, in books, on television, through music. Lies are even present in the church. How are we supposed to recognize the truth? How do we keep from being deceived?

God's Word. Read it. Study it. Memorize it. Live it! It is capable of equipping you for every good work—including lie detection!

Satan wants to do everything in His power to make you believe a lie. He is the master of deception. He wants you to think you are less than worthy. He wants you to doubt God's love for you.

Do you feel insignificant, unworthy, inferior? What lies are you believing today? Whatever you are thinking, challenge each thought with Scripture. Seek out the truth—God's truth found in His perfect Word, the Bible.

Dear Lord, help me not to be deceived by the lies that are
all around me. Help me to know that I am a daughter
of the King and created for a purpose. Thank You for
giving me the truth found in Your Word. Amen.

Does God Laugh?

Whoever would love life and see good days...
1 PETER 3:10

My kids make me laugh. They are so much fun to be around. Have you ever thought about when God laughs? (See Psalm 59:8.) Or does He seem too serious to you? I think God is amused by us, just as we are amused by our children.

Laugh with God. Humor can show the joy of the Christian life. Crass, worldly humor glorifies sin, puts down others, ridicules righteousness, and hurts the spirit, but godly humor encourages people, honors the Lord, and heals the soul.

Admit it—the best source of humor starts at the tip of your nose! The ability to laugh at ourselves is a sign of maturity, of healthy self-esteem, and of having our priorities straight. Author Liz Curtis Higgs tells the true story of a woman who had been given a plant. She watered it, fed it plant food, and even set it outdoors to get sun—only to discover two years later that she had been watering a silk plant! Her family still gets a laugh out of that story today.

We've all been in high-stress situations where we turn to the next person and sigh, "Someday we'll laugh about this." I say, why wait? Lighten up and laugh today!

Dear heavenly Father, fill my life with laughter. Help me to laugh at the good times and the not-so-good times. To laugh at myself for my mistakes and for little things that bring joy. May I remember that I can always rejoice in your salvation. Amen.

Does God Love Me?

What's the price of a pet canary? Some loose change, right?
And God cares what happens to it even more than you do.
He pays even greater attention to you, down to the last
detail...You're worth more than a million canaries.
MATTHEW 10:29-31 MSG

Zits, bad hair days, trying to measure up...being a woman is difficult. We often define ourselves by how we look and what we believe others think of us. We also believe we're successes or failures based on what we do...on our performance as wives, mothers, coworkers, or whatever our roles may be. That way of life is a prescription for disaster.

I have come to believe that most of us don't believe God really loves us. We say we believe He does, yet in our hearts we don't. Think about this: If we really believe God loves us, gifted us to be the way we are, and cares for us more than a cage full of canaries, why do we constantly compare ourselves to others? Comparing leads to coveting—envying others for what they have. And eventually we become angry because our life is less appealing than others'.

The way to stop the cancer of insecurity is to find contentment, to live out the truths of who we are in Christ. Our focus must be on Christ and what He sees in us—that we are fearfully and wonderfully made. Remember, your heavenly Father is enthralled by your beauty (Psalm 45:11). Meditate on those words and on His confidence in you.

O Lord, I praise You for making me so wonderfully. Help me to see
myself in all my glory through Your eyes. Banish my insecurities. Let
my inmost being radiate with Your confidence and love. Amen.

Everything About You

So God created man in his own image, in the image of
God he created him; male and female he created them.
GENESIS 1:27

If you have children, you know that special feeling of rocking them to sleep at night and looking at them—admiring their eyes, their hair, their skin tone, and the shape of their nose. You wonder who they look like, their daddy or their mommy.

Have you ever wondered what it really means to be made in the image of God? Does that mean hair color? Eye color? Height and weight? Or is it more?

It's a lot more. It's about what you have the ability to do and not to do. God enabled you to understand right from wrong. He gave you a free will and the capacity to be in relationships and to honor others by doing what's right. Jesus even said to be perfect as your Father in heaven is perfect (Matthew 5:48).

But often the dreams we have for our own children don't come true because of the choices they make. It's that way with us too. God's dream for our life falls short because of the choices we make.

His dream for you is that you would understand who you are in Him and that you would be like Him in everything you do.

Father, I pray You would help me make wise decisions so
my life is a direct reflection of Your image. Amen.

Facing Adversity

Behold, I am the LORD, the God of all flesh;
is anything too difficult for Me?
JEREMIAH 32:27 NASB

When we are blindsided by the storms of life or face difficult, life-changing circumstances, we can react two ways. We can flee from the pain or face it head-on with extraordinary courage. Pain and adversity can easily strip us of energy and heart. The crippling illness, the war injury, the devastating accident can leave us discouraged and exhausted. We can curse God and flee from Him in our pain, or we can rush toward Him, seeking His shelter and love and holding on tight to His promise that nothing is too hard for Him.

In difficult circumstances and in times of ease, the power of choice and courage is a combination that all extraordinary women wield wisely. Problems are not the real issues in life; rather, what we choose to do with them will determine our future. When the storms rage, press in close to Jesus—He will safely guide your steps and walk with you, even into the valley of the shadow of death. Fear no evil, for He is with you.

O Lord, I pray that You will stay close by my side. Give me courage
to face adversity. Let me find the strength I need to handle any
challenge, any life-altering circumstance that may befall me. Amen.

Facing the Inevitable

For everything there is a season, and a time
for every matter under heaven.
ECCLESIASTES 3:1 NRSV

We are constantly reminded of the inevitability of change. Yet we also tend to get so comfortable that we forget about it. When positive change happens, we allow our emotions to take us to the mountaintop. If all remains good, we get comfortable. Then all of a sudden—*bang!* Something changes, we are thrown into utter shock, and we tumble into the valley.

What has come barreling into your life with no warning? What has drastically changed the way you approach life? What brought you crashing from the mountaintop to the dark valley?

King Solomon learned that there was a time for everything. Life is all about seasons. A season to be happy, a season to be sad. This is why it is so crucial that you place your complete faith in God. You will never know what might be in front of you. Sometimes life makes you laugh, and sometimes it makes you cry. However, God is in control. With this promise, you can wake up each morning ready for what lies ahead!

O Father, help me to understand and accept the inevitable—change happens. Guide me through whatever changes surround my life. Keep me secure in Your love, which is always constant and safe. Amen.

Facing Your Fear

Therefore do not worry about tomorrow, for tomorrow will worry about its own things. Sufficient for the day is its own trouble.

MATTHEW 6:34 NKJV

We're living in uncertain times. We constantly hear about terrorism, economic downturn, unemployment, foreclosure, nuclear armament, identity theft...and that's just the beginning. With so much to be afraid of, it's hard not to worry. We all know what Jesus said about not worrying, but what do we do when the mortgage payment is due and there's no money in the checkbook? Let's face it, in the midst of the fear, refocusing on Christ and realizing that He really does understand what we're going through is just not easy.

When fear begins to creep into your mind and drain your soul, you may lose focus on the One who gives courage. To truly feel His love, we need to remind ourselves that He is the God of the angel armies and that He is called Jehovah Jireh ("The LORD will provide"—Genesis 22:14) for a reason. He does care.

In the face of the fear and unpredictability of our day, you can be certain of one thing—the One who cares for you is God Almighty, the Most High, the Lord of Hosts, Jehovah Jireh. He is the God of the impossible. Nothing is too hard for Him.

Lay your fears at the cross and watch what God will do.

Dear Lord, keep my heart from fear. Let me focus on You, the One who provides. Calm my mind and heart. Replace my fear with comfort, joy, and peace. Amen.

Faith Under Fire

*If anyone suffers as a Christian, let him not be
ashamed, but let him glorify God in this matter.*

1 PETER 4:16 NKJV

Have you ever decided to do something or not to do something
because you chose to obey God instead of going along with the crowd?
Maybe you were with a group of people who were gossiping, and you
decided to walk away. Whatever the circumstance, obedience to God
at that moment seemed to hurt because others didn't respect you for
your decision.

If you have experienced this or are currently facing such times, let
me offer you hope: You are in a perfect position to glorify God. As
Oswald Chambers states, "If we are in love with our Lord, obedience
does not cost us anything; it is a delight, but it costs those who do not
love Him a good deal. If we obey God, it will mean that other people's
plans are upset...we can prevent the suffering; but if we are going to
obey God, we must not prevent it, we must let the cost be paid."

Many times, loyalty to Christ requires us to say no to others. This
can bring about feelings of loneliness and isolation. It is important to
realize that sometimes God allows suffering to come into your life in
order to strengthen your faith. Suffering provides the opportunity to
trust God. You can rejoice because of what God will do in your life
and what He promises for your future! Don't be ashamed, instead,
glorify God!

*Dear Lord, help me to be bold in my faith. Help me not to
get discouraged or defeated when I am persecuted for my
faith. Help me to trust in and depend on You. Amen.*

Faithful in Small Things

Well done, good and faithful servant! You have been faith-
ful with a few things; I will put you in charge of many
things. Come and share your master's happiness!

MATTHEW 25:21

Extraordinary women are faithful in the small things, and that enables God to entrust more to them as they mature and grow in their faith. When we are new in the faith, God usually uses us in small ways. If we are faithful to follow and do His will, He will entrust us to greater goals and achievements, far beyond what we can imagine.

When I was growing up in Montana, I never dreamed God had plans for me to be serving Him the way I am—as president of Extraordinary Women. Standing in front of audiences always unnerved me. It still does. But I've learned that God's dream for my life did not exactly match mine. I'm still amazed when I consider the way God blesses this ministry and empowers me to lead the team of wonderful people who make it all happen. God's dream for me was certainly bigger than the one I had for myself!

Listen carefully to God's voice leading you. Be faithful and follow. He will take your dreams far beyond what you could have ever imagined!

Holy Father, I want to be obedient to Your voice and to follow where
You lead. Help me to be faithful in the tasks You require of me—both
small and great. Test me to see that I am truly worthy of the greater
work You have in store for me. In Jesus' name, I pray. Amen.

Fearfully and Wonderfully Made

I will praise You, for I am fearfully and wonderfully made.
PSALM 139:14 NKJV

When you look in the mirror, what do you see? God's daughter?

Self-hate, rejection, and an inability to accept ourselves as special and unique prevents us from experiencing what God has planned for our lives. Do you feel like a failure? Are you too hard on yourself?

We all need grace. None of us are perfect. But we are made in the image of a great God. It's time to treat yourself better. The Bible says to treat others as you treat yourself, but it starts with treating yourself well! Do something today to remind yourself that you really are fearfully and wonderfully made.

Here's a test. The next time you tell yourself that you're no good, a failure, unlovable—all lies from the devil—ask yourself this one question: *Would I judge a good friend in this way?* If the answer is no, you are not being fair to yourself.

Jesus described God's loving concern for you, explaining that "the very hairs of your head are all numbered." He added that because God cares even for small birds—"not one of them falls to the ground apart from your Father's will"—imagine how much more He cares for you (Matthew 10:29-31 NKJV).

He loves you! Yes—you.

Dear Lord, banish negative thinking from my life. Let me see myself through Your eyes: holy, forgiven, wonderfully made in Your image. Enfold me with Your love so that I am truly beautiful to myself and others. Amen.

Finding Time for Relationships

Come near to God and he will come near to you.
JAMES 4:8

Life is all about relationships. Friends, family, husband, God…each one demands a lot of personal time, energy, and heart. And with online communication and cell phones, you would think we'd somehow be better connected. But we're not! We may be up-to-date with the headlines in each other's lives, but we rarely share about the issues that really matter. But we need those meaningful, deep conversations with one another to gradually create the closeness that we seem to have less and less of.

The lack of relational time, I believe, is a spiritual problem. If the evil one can't make you bad, he'll make you busy. In order to grow in love for others and love for Christ, we must slow down and stay connected to Him. Our verse today says to "come near to God and he will come near to you." We cannot change the number of hours in a day, but we can change the way we spend our time. Be with others. Listen carefully. Have meaningful conversation. Eat a meal together. Make the moments count—especially with your heavenly Father.

Our willingness to give ourselves to others is what really leads to meaningful connection. It builds loyal friendships, trusted family ties, and loving relationships. But loyalty, trust, and love only come when we give ourselves to God and others—over time.

Dear Lord, forgive me for my hurried life. Guide me in how I choose to use my time. Help me to make building relationships with You and others the top priority of my day. Amen.

Fireproof

Fear not, for I have redeemed you; I have summoned you by name; you are mine. When you pass through the waters, I will be with you; and when you pass through the rivers, they will not sweep over you. When you walk through the fire, you will not be burned; the flames will not set you ablaze.

ISAIAH 43:1-2

Did you know that as daughters of God, we are fireproof? That's right, no need for fire alarms that make an excruciating continual beeping noise when the battery needs changing. And no need for flame-retardant pj's either! We are 100 percent flame resistant!

Well, we're flame resistant in the spiritual sense. Think of the fires around you even now: pressures at work, managing your home, taking care of the kids, loss of a loved one, financial strain, marital difficulties. When it comes to the spiritual part of your being, however, nothing can separate you from God and His loving care for you. God promises that He will walk with you every step of the way regardless of what you are going through. You may not always feel as if He is there or that He really cares. Feelings come and go, but the truth of God's Word and His character are unchanging. Although you may feel intense pain emotionally, you can rest in the truth of God's Word that says you will not be consumed by your circumstance. You *can* overcome through Christ!

Dearest Lord, it is such a blessing to know that You will not allow me to be consumed by the fiery trial I am in. Solidify this truth in my heart so I can make it through. To You be the honor and glory for everything in my life! Amen.

Focus on Your Strengths

You show that you are a letter from Christ.

2 CORINTHIANS 3:2

Most of us spend far more time focusing on what we're *not* good at than what we *are* good at. This is the evil one's way of limiting the power and authority you have to proclaim freedom to the captives (Luke 4:18).

Besides, you were born to manifest the glory of God. It's what you were created for. Paul says, "You yourselves are our letter, written on our hearts, known and read by everybody. You show that you are a letter from Christ...written not with ink but with the Spirit of the living God, not on tablets of stone but on tablets of human hearts" (2 Corinthians 3:2-3).

Does the message of your letter shout of Christ's love? Or have you allowed the lies of the enemy to be scribbled in your letter to the world? Lies that say you're too weak, too messed up, too sinful to be used by God?

God wants to use your strength to show Himself to other people through you. When you focus on using your strengths, your light will shine brighter, and your letter will be sent further than you've ever imagined.

Lord, help me to understand the gifts You've given
me, and help me to use them to Your honor and glory
so others will see Your love through me. Amen.

Focused on God's Love

Because of the LORD's great love we are not con-
sumed, for his compassions never fail. They are new
every morning; great is your faithfulness.
LAMENTATION 3:22-23

Tragedy, heartache, and loss—not one of us is immune to times of trouble. Nobody can escape them. The storms of life are inevitable. Life has its way of handing us many blows. And when storms hit, we can feel forsaken and unloved. The question is not whether we'll have storms but rather what we will do with them when they come. Our response to struggles in life will define our attitude toward and confidence in God.

In the midst of trying circumstances, we sometimes allow worry and anger to cloud God's love. That's why we need to respond to the storms with a spirit of faith. Worry keeps us focused on earthly things. Anger, not properly dealt with, keeps us focused on how we'll get even. In both cases, we're focused on something other than God and His everlasting, unconditional love. We must press on in faith, knowing that God will not subject us to more than we can handle.

God's love endures through every struggle, every trial. His dream for us remains strong through the storms of life. Though clouded for the moment by storms, the dreams endure to await the new dawn. Great is His faithfulness toward you!

Dear Lord, let me feel Your presence even when storms roar around
me. Help me to stay firm and secure in the knowledge that Your
love endures forever and that Your compassions never fail. Amen.

Forgiveness

Be kind and compassionate to one another, forgiving each other, just as in Christ God forgave you.
Ephesians 4:32

Forgiving is difficult. Your child is dishonest; a friend betrays you; your boss criticizes you in front of others; your husband lies and has an affair. As a result, you may feel angry and afraid. And if you aren't careful, the pain and anger will give way to resentment and bitterness, eventually destroying you if you won't let go and forgive.

True biblical forgiveness involves applying the grace and forgiveness we receive from Christ to those who've hurt us. Forgiveness frees both the unforgiven and the unforgiving. Though trust and confidence may take time, when we genuinely seek out and act upon forgiveness, we allow for healing and provide the foundation for reconciliation in the relationship. When we forgive, we grow in love. We build trust and create opportunities for healing and intimacy. Healthy relationships demand forgiveness.

Do you need to forgive someone today? God's dream for your life may be hindered by broken relationships. Set aside the offense and never use it as a weapon against the other person. Show grace and forgive. You'll be glad you did!

Dear Lord, let my hardened heart yield to You and forgive those who have hurt or disappointed me. Ease my fear, soothe my anger. Teach me Your way. Amen.

Freedom

The LORD is compassionate and gracious, slow to anger,
abounding in love. He will not always accuse, nor will
he harbor his anger forever; he does not treat us as our
sins deserve or repay us according to our iniquities. For
as high as the heavens are above the earth, so great is his
love for those who fear him; as far as the east is from the
west, so far has he removed our transgressions from us.

PSALM 103:8-12

God's dream for you includes His desire for you to be free. Free from your past sins, your past hurts, or a messed up, reckless lifestyle. He wants to free you from it all. Nothing you ever did and nothing you ever will do disqualifies you from being loved by or used by God.

Just as we must avoid the mistake of believing our shortcomings disqualify us from God's love, we must also avoid the mistake of waiting until we're perfect to seek a deeper relationship with Him. We need Him most when our lives are messy and uncertain. But we don't like to admit our weaknesses, and that often keeps us from approaching our gracious Savior.

Don't wait until the mess is cleaned up to pray. You'll be waiting a very long time! Don't wait until your life is tidy before you share God's love with others. God wants you to come to Him just as you are, right here, right now.

Remember, you are His daughter. In Christ, He has forgiven all your sins. He has wiped the slate clean and is waiting for you to come close to Him. Crawl up into His arms.

Dear Lord, thank You for freeing me from my past.
Help me to let go of the person I once was and to live
freely and joyfully today in Your love. Amen.

Freedom to Risk

But seeing the wind, he became frightened, and beginning to sink, he cried out, "Lord, save me!"
MATTHEW 14:30 NASB

Don't you love a child's heart? Are you touched when you hear their dreams? Ask children what they aspire to be when they grow up, and you'll get an assortment of bold answers. "A race car driver!" "A fireman!" "An American Idol!" Children aren't intimidated by limits or risks. They are determined to reach their dreams.

We are presented with a multitude of challenges throughout our lives, and rarely do those tests ever come without a host of mistakes or even failures. Over time, as the failures pile up, we begin to doubt ourselves. We may even doubt God. Doubt steals away our motivation. A lack of motivation leads to a lack of focus. And eventually we forget our goal.

Sound familiar? Sometimes we can hardly see beyond the present moment and into the promised future.

Has the fear of failure gripped your life? Is the risk too great? Fear makes cowards of all of us. Cry out to the Lord for help in the midst of your fear and step out in faith.

Be a risk taker for Jesus today!

Dear Lord and Savior, help me overcome my fear. Teach me to trust You so I can step out in faith and confidence. Grant me the freedom in You to take any risk necessary to see Your dreams for me fulfilled. Amen.

A Heritage Worth Repeating

He who walks with integrity walks securely.

PROVERBS 10:9 NKJV

*Integrity, character, honesty, living clean...*in a world filled with insider trading, steroid abuse, infidelity, tax evasion, and a myriad of other headline-grabbing flaws, those words seem completely foreign.

Our kids are getting mixed up by the wild messages that bombard them daily. God wants you to teach His commandments to your children with your words and by your example. To talk about God and His commands literally all the time—when sitting, walking, lying down, and getting up. Deuteronomy 6:7 challenges parents to make God's Word a part of every aspect of daily living, even when society fails us. Such demonstrations make it clear to your kids that the Word of God has authority over every area of your life and theirs. Moms, I know you give your children much, but the greatest gift you can give is a godly heritage.

It's still all about integrity, character, honesty, and living clean—and by the way, when you're wrong, admitting it and getting it right again. Live uprightly and walk in your integrity. When you do, you are building a legacy—a heritage worth repeating!

Dear Lord and Father, give me the courage to openly discuss with my children Your words and commandments and the way You want us to live. Guide me as I live out an example of holy living for them. Make every word and action in my day be a testimony of You. Amen.

God's Purpose for You

The LORD will fulfill his purpose for me; your steadfast love, O LORD, endures forever. Do not forsake the work of your hands.

PSALM 138:8 ESV

Have you lost the focus in your life? Are you bogged down in the mundane and the routine? Are you bored and seeking excitement in the wrong places with the wrong people? Does your life seem to have no point or meaning?

Well, I've got some good news for you. Nothing is wasted with God. He uses every moment of every day and every day of every week, month, and year in our lives to fulfill His purpose for us. Times that appear to us to be routine and boring could be times of rest or regrouping to ready us for things we cannot imagine. Hectic times when we are hurting may be training grounds for understanding what lies ahead. Times when we are downright gleeful and filled with joy refresh and renew our lives and our love for the Lord. All that we do fits within God's plan and purpose for our lives. No action is too small. No thought is too insignificant for God to notice and to use for His good.

Delight in God's love. Be reassured by His faithfulness to a thousand generations that have come before us. His love endures forever, and nothing can ever change His wonderful plans for His people and for you!

Dear Lord and Father, thank You for being so loving and faithful to Your people for a thousand generations. Let me rest in the assurance that You will fulfill all that You have planned for my life. Amen.

God's Waitress

Each one should use whatever gift he has received to serve others,
faithfully administering God's grace in its various forms.
1 PETER 4:10

God has given each of us, by His grace, a gift—a spiritual gift. And since we have received the gift by grace, we are to use it in service to others. I've heard this concept compared to a waitress at a restaurant. When a waitress offers food to guests, she's not prideful because she didn't prepare the food. She doesn't think of keeping the food for herself because it wasn't prepared for her. Her role is to enjoy the honor of carrying the food from the chef to the diners. In the same way, God gives us spiritual gifts so we can distribute them to His people. We are God's representatives, the picture of His grace to those around us. What a privilege!

As we disperse the spiritual gifts God has so graciously given to us, let us keep in mind the ultimate goal, found in 1 Peter 4:11, "that in all things God may be praised through Jesus Christ. To him be the glory and the power for ever and ever. Amen."

Dear Lord, thank You for the gifts You have given me. May I
humbly use them in Your service to others. Help me to become
like a waitress who is honored to serve others. Amen.

Grow in Grace

*All this is for your benefit, so that the grace that is reaching more
and more people may cause thanksgiving to overflow to the glory
of God. Therefore we do not lose heart. Though outwardly we are
wasting away, yet inwardly we are being renewed day by day.*

2 Corinthians 4:15-16

Grace is one of the most beautiful words I have ever heard. If someone were to describe me, I hope she would include the word *grace*.

Grace is a quality pleasing for its charm. Grace is attractive. Desirable. An unmerited favor. Grace is a favor rendered by one who does not need to do so. God is grace—in every sense of the word. And His grace is sufficient for your every need (2 Corinthians 12:9).

Think of someone you know who is full of grace. I imagine someone who gives without reservation and loves unconditionally.

God's dream for you is to become more like Christ and reflect "the grace that is reaching more and more people." Growing in grace requires that you have a relationship with the God of all grace. Through daily Bible reading and communion with Him, grace will be evident in your life.

*Dear Lord, thank You for showing grace to me when
there was no reason to do so. Develop grace in my life
so that others may be drawn to You. Amen.*

Hats Off

The king is enthralled by your beauty;
honor him, for he is your lord.

PSALM 45:11

Have you ever looked in the mirror at crazy hair? You become frustrated, aggravated, and tense. You're not going to resign yourself to a bad hair day; instead, you put on a hat. Or have you looked out the window and into gloomy, cold weather? You realize you need some kind of protection for your head and decide it's a hat day.

In the past, women wore hats to display their social status. In biblical times, scribes and the Pharisees and other religious personnel wore hats in accordance to their laws. Often the word *hat* is used as a metaphor referring to the different roles we have as women, like the hat of motherhood or the hat of being a wife. But sometimes we use hats to hide what we do not want others to see.

Many times, we as women feel the need to cover up all of our imperfections and flaws in order to be accepted by others and succeed in life. But God sees you as you are—and He loves you. Just listen to His unconditional love: "The LORD said to Samuel, 'Do not consider his appearance or his height, for I have rejected him. The LORD does not look at the things man looks at. Man looks at the outward appearance, but the LORD looks at the heart'" (1 Samuel 16:7). God simply wants us to come to Him, just as we are—and most importantly, He wants your heart. Uncover it and give it to Him.

Dear Lord, thank You for loving me just the way I am. Help me
to see myself through Your loving eyes today and always. Amen.

He Must Increase

He must increase, but I must decrease.
JOHN 3:30 NKJV

When people—your kids, family, friends—look at you, what do they see? How would they describe you? What words would they use? *Kind? Gentle? Loving? Grouchy? Distant? Busy? Christlike?*

Think of life this way—God has given your spouse to you because He wants to work through you to make *him* more like *Him* (Jesus). God has given your kids to you because He wants to work through you to make *them* more like *Him*. It's amazing what happens when we stop and let Christ work in and through us. Our relationships change and are graced.

God's will is for you to give way to Jesus in all His glory, to help others fix their eyes on Him in adoration of all He is. Let this be a new day…and a new you.

Dear Lord, help me to humbly walk with You and let Your light shine through me so that You receive glory for all I say and do. Help me not to get in the way of what You want to accomplish in my life. Amen.

Heroes

For even the Son of Man did not come to be served, but
to serve, and to give His life as a ransom for many.

Mark 10:45

Heroes come in all shapes and sizes: male, female, young, old, tall, short, famous, common…just to name a few. Some people would say their hero is a family member or friend. For others, their hero is a celebrity or a famous athlete.

In the military, the Purple Heart is given when a soldier is wounded or killed in action. He is honored and considered a hero. The fireman who races into a burning building to save lives is a hero. The mother who picks her child up after a fall is a hero.

There are heroes in the nursery at your church, in your child's classroom, at the local homeless shelter in your community, at the teen pregnancy center…heroes are everywhere!

Just look in the mirror. Because God became your Hero, you can be a hero too! When you feel weak and vulnerable, He is your strength and a safe haven. When you need rescuing from the craziness of life, He will provide for your needs. He is truly the ultimate Hero! And we are heroes too when we let Him do His work in and through us every day.

Dear Lord, when I am weak, You are strong—and
I am grateful for that. Thank You for sustaining me
through difficult times. You are my Hero! Amen.

His Presence in Hard Times

Even though I walk through the valley of the shadow of death...
PSALM 23:4

Loss is a part of life. This is difficult to admit, but it's true. Facing reality honestly helps us grow. We must find a way to face losses, grieve, and begin a process of healing.

That's why I believe God carefully places crucial Scripture into our hearts, especially during times of loss and heartache. Psalm 23 was a refuge for me when I lost my father. God reminds us of His presence both now and for eternity. Because of Jesus, we as Christians can experience simultaneous emotions of sorrow and joy.

Part of me asks, *God, why is Dad gone?* The other part says, *I will see him again.* Sorrow and joy together at the same time—because of what Christ did on the cross.

When hard times hit, know that Jesus will restore your soul. He will guide you in paths of righteousness. And even though you walk through the valley of the shadow of death, He walks with you.

Sorrow is a part of life, but so is our hope in Christ. That's the assurance that gives us strength and allows us to find joy in the morning.

Father, thank You for walking with me in my sorrows. I pray today that goodness and love will follow me and that I will dwell in the house of the Lord forever. Amen.

Hopefully Devoted

Acknowledge the God of your father, and serve him with wholehearted devotion and with a willing mind, for the LORD searches every heart and understands every motive behind the thoughts. If you seek him, he will be found by you.

1 CHRONICLES 28:9

I know I'm getting older now, but most of you can probably hum with me a few lines from the hit song in *Grease* called "Hopelessly Devoted." I can still hear Sandy singing to her beloved Danny about her total devotion to him.

Ah, love songs. One love-stricken person pouring out her heart to another. It's what most of us desire—to be madly in love with someone who is loyal, faithful, and devoted. Some, however, are so smitten by the concept or idea of love that they will give themselves to anything and even compromise who they are and what they stand for. They hold tight to the idea of love because it sounds better than having no relationship at all. I find it sad to watch women give themselves to relationships that have no hope just because they are desperate for love.

The God of the universe "knows the secrets of [your] heart" (Psalm 44:21). He knows the motives behind your thoughts. And He tells you that if you seek Him, you will find Him. He is "good to those whose hope is in Him" (Lamentations 3:25). No man will ever fulfill the desperate longings of your heart. Only One can do that—Jesus.

God's dream for you is to be hopefully devoted to Jesus. Are you?

Father, I admit that sometimes, following You is hard. I pray today that You will teach me how to be devoted wholeheartedly to You. Amen.

Hospitality

Share with God's people who are in need. Practice hospitality.
ROMANS 12:13

I love the holidays—especially Christmas. I enjoy spending time with family and friends. It's so much fun to get together with those we love. Laughing, sharing, the warmth of the fireplace...just thinking about these things brings me joy.

But the real blessing comes when we are able to give to someone who's in need. When we do, we are the ones who receive the greater blessing. That's God's gift to those who give!

An elderly lady beams with joy because someone decided to clean her home...a young family is able to pay off a debt due to an anonymous financial gift...a single mom gets a night off because someone offered to watch her kids...these are examples of true hospitality. And this kind of giving touches the heart of God.

When was the last time you reached out and touched someone? Look around your neighborhood. Talk with the leaders of your church about needs within the congregation. Visit a local nursing facility or homeless shelter. Serve as a volunteer at a crisis pregnancy center. Call a friend. Smile at someone. There are millions of ways to practice hospitality. God wants to use you today!

Dear Lord, open my eyes and heart to people around me who are in need. Give me a desire to practice hospitality daily! Amen.

In His Presence

"Now therefore, I pray, if I have found grace in Your sight, show me now Your way, that I may know You and that I may find grace in Your sight. And consider that this nation is Your people." And [the Lord] said, "My Presence will go with you, and I will give you rest." Then [Moses] said to Him, "If Your Presence does not go with us, do not bring us up from here."

EXODUS 33:13-15 NKJV

I love this dialogue! Moses says to the Lord, "Show me *Your* way," not "Look at my way; this is the way I want to go." In fact, he continues by telling the Lord, "If You do not go with us, I want no part of it. I only want to be where you are." So many times, prayers are offered asking God to bless the steps we have chosen for our lives. Rather, we should change our hearts to desire to stay with God instead of asking Him to stay with us. We can ask Him to teach us, to show us His way. Herein lays the key to consistency with the Lord.

If we are following the Lord instead of asking Him to follow us around, we can enjoy the assurance of His presence in our lives. There is inexpressible freedom in allowing the Lord to have control of our decisions and the direction of our lives. May I both encourage and challenge you to speak candidly with the Lord today. Walk in His presence rather than expecting Him to walk in yours.

Dear Lord, thank You for guiding me through life even when I stray my own way. I pray today, Father, that You will be a guiding light for me and that I will submit to Your way and surrender my own. Help me, Lord, to discover and follow Your plans. I pray in Jesus' name. Amen.

In Season and Out of Season

Be prepared in season and out of season.
2 Timothy 4:2

Seasons change. Sometimes our skies are blue, the birds sing, the sun warms our spirits, and we are filled with such joy that we nearly burst from the sheer blessing of being alive. Those times can quickly fade though, and we are sometimes left with chilling pain and questions about today or tomorrow.

Paul encouraged Timothy to be prepared in season and out of season, to be ready to share the gospel message with anyone at any time. However, we can also apply this verse to all areas of our lives. Be ready with a game plan for when the tough seasons come. I know that it's impossible to be fully prepared for the pain that enters your life, especially the unexpected. Staying connected to God and other believers is the best way to build the support you need to endure the unwanted seasons that will come.

What season of life are you in today? I want you to know that my heart is reaching out to you. I encourage you with the strong and steadfast promise that He is exactly what you need today, tomorrow, and in every season of the rest of your days!

Dear Lord, prepare my heart for each season of life that comes.
Help me to remain close to You and to build relationships
with other believers I can trust and lean on in times of
need. Help me to be that kind of friend as well. Amen.

In the Center of Circumstances

For you, O God, tested us; you refined us like silver.

PSALM 66:10

The Refiner's fire is necessary to remove the impurities and produce a renewed strength and elegance in us. But fire equals pain, and pain hurts. Sometimes it hurts so badly we miss what's waiting for us on the other side of the sorrow, heartache, and unhappiness. Instead, we walk gingerly through life so we don't have to feel anything too deeply.

The refiner usually sits by the fire, watches, and waits. How does he know when the metal is pure? When he can see his reflection.

Next time you hurt, know that God is sitting right there beside you. He'll see you through as soon as He can see His reflection in you!

You can get to the next level and live God's dream for you by discovering where you feel resistant in your life and then identifying what you can learn from it. Those courageous enough to meet Him in the midst of their circumstances, whatever they may be, have the guarantee of His provision. By surrendering to Him, we show a willingness to grow through even our unwanted circumstances. The moment we yield is the instant healing begins.

Dear Lord and Father, use the circumstances of my life to refine me. Make me purer and more loving. Let me cling to You and draw nearer to You regardless of the circumstances in my life. Amen.

Intrusion

*Come to me, all you who are weary and bur-
dened, and I will give you rest.*
MATTHEW 11:28

Do you ever come home to find total chaos and wonder whether
intruders came into your home? Have you wondered if your family
has completely forgotten any civilized way of living that you may
have taught them? Maybe you've asked yourself, *Does anyone around
this house get it? Does anyone appreciate what it takes to keep up and get
everything done?* For a moment you may even wonder if the only way
to prevent chaos is to actually stay home 24/7.

During these moments it's easy to feel invisible, underappreciated,
and angry. Know that Jesus is in touch with the burdens of life that
you carry. He knows how much they hurt and exhaust you, draining
your desire to know Him and realize His dreams for you. But when
you give your troubled heart to Him, He gives you rest for your soul.
His gift is the kind of rest that will cure burnout and renew your
enthusiasm for Him! It may not help clean the house, but it will keep
you from strangling someone!

*Dear Lord, when my life is in chaos and everything I have
to do seems like a heavy burden, help me. Remind me that
I can leave my concerns with You and find rest. Amen.*

Jesus Prays for You

Now this is eternal life: that they may know you, the only
true God, and Jesus Christ, whom you have sent.

JOHN 17:3

The verse for today is part of a prayer that Jesus prayed to God the Father after His last supper with His disciples. Moments prior to Jesus' arrest, we see Him in the garden, praying for us—praying for you! His primary concern was that we would know that He is the way to eternal life. Oh, what a beautiful kind of love!

Jesus still prays for you today! "Christ Jesus, who died—more than that, who was raised to life—is at the right hand of God and is also interceding for us" (Romans 8:34). He is praying for you!

Have you ever felt as if your prayers only reach to the ceiling? Does God seem to be distant—a faraway, heavenly diety who cannot be reached? Have you ever felt as if no one cares, no one understands? God's dream for you is to understand how much He loves you and to know that Jesus is praying for you right now! "God is our refuge and strength, an ever-present help in trouble" (Psalm 46:1). He is always there, always praying, always interceding on your behalf. Be encouraged today—you are loved and prayed for!

Dear Lord, thank You for thinking about me. Thank You for
praying for me on my behalf. Help me to let others know that You
have the same love for them and desire that they know You. Amen.

Joy Gone Awry

*Now the Lord had prepared a great fish to swallow Jonah. And
Jonah was in the belly of the fish three days and three nights.*

JONAH 1:17 NKJV

If you are married, think back to your wedding day for a moment.
If you're not married, dream ahead with me. Picture what it was like
or what it would be like to have your sister or maid of honor fixing
your hair and giggling with you in the dressing room. Picture yourself
walking down the aisle, looking at the handsome groom awaiting your
beautiful countenance.

What feelings have surfaced within you? Joy? Excitement? Exhila-
ration? Or maybe anger? Frustration? Sadness? Unfortunately for some
people, a day that was supposed to be a completely joyous occasion
that led to happiness has resulted in pain and heartache.

Jonah experienced an absence of joy. The absence of joy can ruin
the memories of what is supposed to be beautiful. After Jonah dis-
obeyed God, a great fish swallowed him up for three days. God's
mercy forced the fish to spit him out. Even after this experience, Jonah
was angry with God for saving Nineveh. Jonah's motives are hard to
decipher from the text, but we can safely say that his motives were
self-centered.

I pray for joy to fill your life. Do not allow self-centeredness or
a lack of focus on the significant things cause the joy in your life to
go awry. May your joy be found in the significance of our Lord and
Savior, Jesus Christ.

*Dear Lord, help me to have true joy. I know I may not
always feel happy, but I can still have joy. Help me to
remain focused on what really matters in life. Amen.*

Joyful Bad Times

But let all who take refuge in you be glad; let them
ever sing for joy. Spread your protection over them,
that those who love your name may rejoice in you.

PSALM 5:11

How is it that we can experience joy in times of pain?

That's because joy and happiness are not synonymous. Joy does not depend on our circumstances, but happiness does. We can go through the ups and downs of life, the good times and bad, continuing to remain joyful.

Where can we find joy when we want our life circumstances fixed or healed—yesterday?

When we are in the midst of a painful circumstance, we sometimes struggle to find hope, to see the light at the end of the tunnel. But there's good news! God promises us that if we stay obedient to Him, the product of suffering is perseverance and character. These attributes produce hope.

There is purpose in your pain, in your trial, in those hard times. I know, I hate those times too! But our sufferings do change us. They shape our hearts.

So pray for joy in the midst of the suffering. After all, "God has poured out his love into our hearts by the Holy Spirit, whom he has given us" (Romans 5:5). This promise is sealed with the Holy Spirit, so you do not have to be discouraged by your sufferings. There is hope!

Dear Lord Jesus, You are my hope giver. In times of suffering
and difficulty in this life, show me Your joy, Your light, Your
hope. Give me renewed courage to face my circumstances as I
stay focused on Your love and Your dream for my life. Amen.

Thank-You Notes

*Continue to live in him, rooted and built up
in him, strengthened in the faith as you were
taught, and overflowing with thankfulness.*

COLOSSIANS 2:6-7

Isn't it so much fun to receive a thank-you note? So many different types of thank-you notes have been designed. Many are simple and sweet, colorful and full of zest, with stripes and polka dots, flowers and scenic landscapes, and so much more! And the note itself is written from the thankful heart of the writer. A note that exclaims you are appreciated and you are noticed!

Have you ever made a list of the things you are thankful for? If not, I encourage you to begin that list today. You will be amazed at how your mood will be uplifted. Counting your blessings is a sure way to take your eyes off the things that appear to be going wrong and to focus them on what is right. After making the list, invest a dollar or two in a card or note. Then write a thank-you note to God! Everything that you have to be thankful for came from your loving and generous God. Just the fact that you are reading this devotional means that God has given you life for today! Thank Him and praise Him.

*Dear Lord, thank You! When I get bogged down with life, help
me to remember what I have and to count my blessings. You are
worthy of all praise, and without You, I am nothing. Amen.*

That Special Day

For the day of the LORD is near in the valley of decision.

JOEL 3:14

Think back for a moment to the last time you were anticipating a special day—a big family vacation, graduation day, the last day of school, your child's birthday, Christmas morning...

Special days filled with wonder, adventure, spontaneity, honor, blessing, and love are priceless. They create the memories that bind us with loved ones as years go by. But these pale in comparison to a very special day that all believers of Jesus Christ anticipate. The prophet Joel calls it "the day of the Lord." He says that in that day, "the LORD will be a refuge for his people" (Joel 3:16). What a wonderful mental picture—we will one day be sheltered by the Lord! God promised to restore Judah and bring about a time of unparalleled material and spiritual blessing (Joel 2:18-32; 3:18-21).

If we belong to Christ, we can look forward to the day of the Lord with great anticipation. It will be a day like no other! With this coming day we can rejoice together as we "praise the name of the LORD...who has worked wonders for you; never again will my people be shamed (Joel 2:26).

Jesus came to take away your shame, to clothe you with His righteousness. His coming is near. Be washed clean and ready for His return.

Dear Lord, I can't wait until Your coming. I wait with eager anticipation to see Your face. Help me to share this excitement with others who may not know You. Amen.

The Hands of Jesus

Be kind and compassionate to one another.
EPHESIANS 4:32

Have you ever had a colleague offer a tissue in response to your tears? A neighbor you've never met bring dinner over when she learns your mother passed away? A friend offer to keep your young children so you can fly out to your grandma's funeral? They might not all be Christians, but they are Jesus' hands and feet in dark hours.

All too often, we're uncomfortable letting anyone know that all is not right in our world. We don't want to owe anyone, so we hesitate to accept the help that comes in response to tough times.

But Jesus reaches down from heaven through other people's hands. When we refuse their help, we may actually be refusing Him. We cry out for God's help, but when it comes in the form of another human, we are loath to accept it. For some reason we suddenly let pride stand in the way of allowing God to use other people to show us His love and compassion.

If you're in the midst of tough times right now, how can you let others use their hands to be Jesus to you? Can you accept a meal? An offer of transportation? A willingness to run errands? By saying yes, you'll let Jesus comfort you through the people He's placed specifically and purposefully in your life. Allow Him to serve you.

O Lord Jesus, let me see Your face in the concerned expression of a neighbor who brings me a meal. Let me feel Your arms in the arms of others who give me hugs of reassurance. Let my heart be open to receiving Your love through the people You have put in my life. Amen.

The Importance of Being a Teacher

*Come, my children, listen to me; I will
teach you the fear of the LORD.*

PSALM 34:11

A thunderous crash, a booming thud, a screeching howl...the kids are at it again. The brightly decorated playroom has been transformed into a war zone of exasperation and vexation between siblings. Sound familiar?

I would imagine every parent who has more than one child could describe similar scenes. In fact, if you have siblings, you could probably relate your own accounts of childhood skirmishes. Disagreements between children are typical, and they help kids develop skills for resolving conflict. But what happens when those skills are not taught and refined within their character development?

No price tag can be placed on the value of equipping your children with the tools to make positive choices, to love each other, and to resolve conflict successfully and biblically. As a parent, you are reproducing not only biologically, but experientially.

Teaching the leaders of tomorrow is a high calling and honor. Even if you don't have children in your life, someone is always watching what you do. Opportunities to teach others about the God you serve are all around you. Learn to see those open doors, and be courageous and teach others the way!

*Dear Lord, help me to be a teacher. I want to help others
understand what it means to fear, honor, and respect You. Help
me to see the opportunities You place before me. Amen.*

The Longings of a Father

The LORD longs to be gracious to you; he rises to show you compassion. For the LORD is a God of justice. Blessed are all who wait for him!

ISAIAH 30:18

Did you know that God the Father longs for you? In fact, He longs to be *gracious* to you! He is constantly finding ways to shower you with compassionate love. A love like that does not exist anywhere but in the character of God.

I love my kids. I enjoy showering them with my love in many ways. Providing, protecting, counseling, instructing, disciplining… these are all ways that I work to love them. Sometimes they notice, sometimes they don't.

I am certainly not perfect, and I can't say that I have loved my kids perfectly. Sin continues to affect my judgment if I am not careful. I am so glad I have an example to follow in God the Father. He never gives up. His love never fails!

You may be struggling with a wayward child who sometimes seems impossible to love. Or your own parents may never have shown love to you. Rest in Isaiah 30:18, and know that your Father in heaven longs to be gracious to you—right now!

Dear Lord, thank You for loving me. It is a comfort to know that I am longed for…and loved! Amen.

The Lord Within

*Not that we are sufficient of ourselves to think of anything
as being from ourselves, but our sufficiency is from God.*

2 Corinthians 3:5 nkjv

My son, Zach, looks a lot like his dad. And of course, they both love sports—especially baseball. Tim has pretty much coached Zach since he was four years old. One thing I learned as a mom was that Zach had to hit, field, catch, and throw the baseball on his own. Tim couldn't do it for him. In order to learn, Zach had to do it alone.

Even still, Tim will always be there cheering and coaching Zach whenever and wherever he needs him.

The Lord calls each of us to do infinitely more than we can even imagine. He also teaches us, through His Word, how to accomplish the things He has called us to do.

Your effectiveness and success in your family, work, ministry, and relationship with the Lord depend on His grace and His sufficiency. God is your coach! But you have to get in the game. When you do, know that He is always there, cheering you on to do great things for His kingdom!

*Heavenly Father, I am tired of trying to live each day by the power
of my own self-sufficiency. I confess that I cannot do it on my own
and that I need Your grace and sufficiency within me. I invite
You now into my daily rounds. Teach me, O Lord, to rely on Your
strength, and may I be completely energized by You. Thank You for
freely offering Your strength to me. I receive it now and ask that You
help me to rely on You. I ask these things in Jesus' name. Amen.*

The One Who Dwells Within

I will pray the Father, and He will give you another Helper, that
He may abide with you forever—the Spirit of truth, whom the
world cannot receive, because it neither sees Him nor knows Him;
but you know Him, for He dwells with you and will be in you.

JOHN 14:16-17 NKJV

Ever wonder what it means to truly have the Holy Spirit living within you? It can be a strange thought, but comforting nonetheless.

As the passage in John tells us, we know the Holy Spirit, we recognize and have a relationship with Him, because He dwells with us and will be in us. These words present a mental picture to me of the Holy Spirit not only living within us, guiding and directing us, but also walking beside us, holding our hand along the way. He is the manifestation of God's "ever-present help in trouble" (Psalm 46:1).

Whether you are on a crowded city street or on a deserted island with no one else present, you are never alone. Many times, the loneliness you experience is the result of simply not acknowledging who is already there. Acknowledge Him, and He will be there even now. You always have an audience of One!

Father, thank You for always being there for me. Help me to know
that I am not alone. Holy Spirit, walk with me and dwell in me
as I seek to become one with You. As I abide in You, may my
feelings of loneliness be overcome by the beauty of solitude. Amen.

The Path of Patience

*Let patience have its perfect work, that you may
be perfect and complete, lacking nothing.*

JAMES 1:4 NKJV

Many of us have forgotten the path of patience we must take to get to the next level in our relationship with Christ. It has been rejected by a society thriving on instant gratification, faster technology, and a fear of commitment. We want it now, or we don't want it at all. Even committing to a two-year cell phone agreement is considered a courageous feat these days. No wonder we balk when we hear the word *patience*. Our culture has denied it, and most of us have forgotten it.

To discover God's dream for our lives, we've got to rediscover the forgotten path. Surely the path is paved with patience, so if you live your life constantly trying other routes, hoping that a quick devotion in the morning and a ten-second prayer for your neighbor with cancer will get you to the next level, you're likely to grow frustrated and resentful. We learn patience as we embrace tough times.

When you're facing difficult times, remember the hope found in the Easter story. Life can come after loss, and we can bear it because of Christ. The question isn't whether you will have tragedy and loss in your life. Those are givens. The question is, what will you decide to do with it? Will it take you under? Will it make you stronger? Will it take you deeper? Will you allow God to use it for His glory?

*Teach me patience, Lord—patience to endure hard
times and loss, patience to see that difficulties draw me
nearer to You. Bring me to a higher level of relationship
with You through the tough times in life. Amen.*

The Power of Influence

Finally, brothers, whatever is true, whatever is noble,
whatever is right, whatever is pure, whatever is lovely,
whatever is admirable—if anything is excellent
or praiseworthy—think about such things.

PHILIPPIANS 4:8

Do your relationships empower you to think about positive things? Do they lift you up? Brighten your spirits? Or do they cause you worry, despair, and anxiety? Some people may have a negative influence on us, some a positive one. We struggle with relationships that burn us out, leaving us drained and discouraged. *After all,* we tell ourselves, *maybe I can be a positive influence on her.* But we have to ask ourselves, *Am I having a greater influence on her than her negativity is having on me?* You have to find balance and be wise when choosing whom to spend time with.

On the other hand, you never know who may come to faith in Christ because of the life you live or because of your friendship. You can't force faith on someone else, so you must simply be willing to live out your own testimony and answer questions that naturally arise. God will do His work.

You will become like the people you spend time with. You influence the lives of others, but you also need to let Christ minister to you through them. Who is influencing you?

Lord, let me be a positive influence on others. Give me
discretion to know when to befriend someone and when
to let go of a relationship that is a negative influence
on my life. In Christ's name I ask this. Amen.

The Secret to Contentment

I have learned the secret of being content in any and every situation, whether well fed or hungry, whether living in plenty or in want. I can do everything through him who gives me strength.

PHILIPPIANS 4:12-13

Content—it literally means to desire no more than what one has, or to be satisfied. Do you know anybody who lives with such freedom? Content. Satisfied. Settled. Fun to be around. Free.

Despite the hardships and painful circumstances he endured, the apostle Paul remained content. He was confident in Jesus and recognized that his strength came from the Lord. He learned the secret of being content in any and every situation. And God wants to reveal the same secret to you. He wants you to be content with your life and with the assignments you're given, trusting God's strength to make it possible.

But as you and I both know, being content is not easy. When money is tight, when your kids are out of control, when your boss is demanding too much, when your husband is being, well, you know... life circumstances can bring about discontent.

Use this situation to your advantage. It is probably a sign that God wants to take you deeper still. He wants you to learn that though life is tough, He's present in your anger, fear, insecurity, and depression. He's your strength when you feel the job is too big or you can't go on. Rest in Him and discover the contentment that only the Holy Spirit can give.

Dear Lord, teach me to be content regardless of the stage or state of life I am in. Let me count the blessings You have showered on me and find contentment in knowing I am truly blessed. Amen.

The Spirit of Truth

But when he, the Spirit of truth, comes,
he will guide you into all truth.

JOHN 16:13

Have you ever found yourself wishing the Lord would suddenly appear in your living room with step-by-step instructions for your life? Perhaps you've thought, *If God can speak directly to Abraham, Moses, Mary, and Paul, why not me?*

Sometimes it's hard to believe in what we can't see. Sometimes it's hard to trust the untouchable. I've learned, however, that Christ works in and through me, guiding my desires and decisions by the power of the Holy Spirit.

He's called the Spirit of truth. He makes God's Word come alive in our hearts and helps us put it to work in our marriages, families, and careers. All of us have missed His leading at one time or another by not seeking His guidance. We stomp our foot and defiantly demand, "Our will be done!" rather than saying, "Your will be done." But God's will is best for us—it is His dream for our lives. Yielding to it will be better than any adventure we can ever imagine.

Extraordinary woman, let the gentle Holy Spirit nurture you in love and truth today. Look to the sky—not wanting more *from* God, but more *of* God.

O Holy One, help me to willingly yield to Your direction
and Your purpose for my life. Fill me with the desire
to seek You and follow Your guidance in every step I
take. In your Son's precious name, I pray. Amen.

Squirrels, Nuts, and Faith

If you have faith as small as a mustard seed, you can say to
this mountain, "Move from here to there" and it will move.
MATTHEW 17:20

At our home in Virginia, squirrels run and jump from tree to tree all year long, scurrying around to find that precious nut. God has definitely given them a great work ethic, strength, and determination. The squirrel, with the ability to persevere and stay motivated toward the goal, always gets the nut.

So many times, we struggle to stay motivated and persevere through the day-to-day tasks that are before us. We do the laundry, cook, clean, change diapers, provide taxi service for the children, pay bills, organize a home, grocery shop, clip coupons, work in the office, feed the family pet, take care of aging parents, and so much more, day in and day out. Where can we find motivation to continue persevering toward the end goal and dream God has given us?

It's found in our faith. Scripture tells us that by faith, Moses "left Egypt...he persevered because he saw him who is invisible. By faith he kept the Passover" (Hebrews 11:27-28). Moses was a man of perseverance, but most of all, a man of faith.

We must have faith if we want to persevere. Faith that God is who He says He is—a rewarder of those who diligently seek after His will for their lives. Let me encourage you to keep on keeping on for His glory and for that eternal crown that you will be able to lay at the Savior's precious feet while hearing Him say, "Well done!"

Dear Lord, help me today to be like the squirrel—diligent,
motivated, determined, and steadfast. Build my faith in
You and in Your ability to direct my steps. Amen.

The Trust Fall

*Trust in him at all times, O people; pour out
your hearts to him, for God is our refuge.*

PSALM 62:8

Trusting God to reveal His dream in your life and give you hope often requires an extraordinary act of willpower. It's kind of like one of those "trust falls," where you fall backward into the arms of someone you trust to catch you. You give up total control and place absolute trust in that person to catch you in that moment.

God wants to teach you the same about Him—that you're not in control. He is. He wants to show you that when He seems most absent and you're falling backward, He really is most present and there to catch you. God walks beside you even when you can't see, hear, or feel Him. He provides you with what you need to get through deep pain, unbelievable circumstances, and surreal events. In your weakness, He wants you to fall backward, into His arms. Place your trust in Him and let Him prove to you that He will not disappoint.

*Lord, let my trust in You grow to the point that I can lean on You
in absolute confidence even when the worst is happening in my life.
Stand firm and secure behind me whenever I'm about to fall. Amen.*

The Truth of Spiritual Warfare

Nevertheless do not rejoice in this, that the spirits are subject to you, but rather rejoice because your names are written in heaven.

LUKE 10:20 NKJV

From the time sin entered the world, wars have been fought for a wide variety of reasons. Nations have waged world wars because ruthless leaders carried out acts of genocide, and today war rages across various parts of the world between terror cells and the countries seeking to destroy them. War is inevitable and will continue.

The same holds true in your spiritual life. Continuous war must be fought by believers. The war I am talking about is the constant struggle between good and evil as Satan tries to rule your life. Broken relationships, loss of jobs, constant conflicts in your marriage, lies you believe about yourself...these can all be related to Satan's attack on you!

What battles are you facing? What lies do you believe from the enemy? In Luke 10, Jesus grants the disciples and all believers, including you, the power not only to overcome evil but to trample on forces of wickedness so that "nothing shall by any means hurt you" (Luke 20:19 NKJV). Jesus has already defeated Satan and has won this battle through His death and resurrection. Because of His sacrifice, you can have eternal life, and your name written in heaven. Regardless of what you are facing, you are victorious through Christ! We don't fight *for* victory in Christ, but *from* our victory in Him.

Dear Lord, I am so glad You have won the victory over Satan. Help me to remember that I am victorious, in any battle that I am facing, through You and Your mighty power! Amen.

To: You
From: God

*Now about spiritual gifts, brothers, I do
not want you to be ignorant.*

1 Corinthians 12:1

The Lord wants us to clearly know that He has given every believer spiritual gifts. It's as if He doesn't want to leave us any room to say, "I really would serve You if I could, but I just don't have anything to offer." By the power of the Holy Spirit within us, He has given each one of us unique gifts that enable us to build up the church and glorify Him.

So what are these gifts?

Romans 12, 1 Corinthians 12, and Ephesians 4 list quite a few, including administration, giving, helping, teaching, evangelism, and mercy. God gives each individual a different combination of these spiritual gifts. As we grow in Him, the gifts we have will develop and mature.

God has a plan. He is not willing that any should perish but that all would enjoy a life in Him. God has gifted you with everything you need to serve Him, so you can trust that others will see your good works and glorify your Father in heaven. Do it wholeheartedly. Give Him the glory for all He is doing in and through you!

*O Lord, the Giver of Gifts, thank You for the gifts You
have given me. Help me to recognize my unique gifts so I
can use them wholeheartedly in Your service. Amen.*

Tranquility and God's Sovereignty

Better one handful with tranquility than two hand-
fuls with toil and chasing after the wind.

ECCLESIASTES 4:6

Tranquility—a little peace and quiet—I need more of it. Do you? For the average American woman, rest has become an elusive dream. More often than not we are stressed with the double burden of working a full-time job and taking care of family. For most it is pretty overwhelming and exhausting. When we finally do have the time to relax, we are annoyed by the thoughts of what has not yet been done.

Stop. Take a breath. Learn to rely on God to help you make it through your day. He promises not to give you more than you can handle. Be sure to understand and discern what you may be trying to handle beyond what God is asking you to do.

As the day progresses, cast your burdens and worries onto Him. "Better one handful with tranquility than two handfuls with toil." King Solomon reminds us that worry is meaningless. God will still be sovereign even if you do not have time today to finish what can wait for tomorrow. Relax in His perfect peace.

O Sovereign Lord, my Prince of perfect peace, when my
life gets to hectic and frazzled, shower me with Your
peace and tranquility. Let my mind and spirit find
rest in You to help me through my day. Amen.

Trusting God's Love

No one has ever seen God; but if we love one another,
God lives in us and his love is made complete in us.

1 John 4:12

From time to time we lack security. We don't feel safe. We can even wonder, *Does God really love me? How could He, after all I've done?* When the trials of life press in, He often seems even further away. Welcome to the danger zone. It's where the evil one whispers lies in your ear. He tells you that love can't be trusted. He says that God is far away and really doesn't care.

But here is where God is at His best. He sends little reminders that He can be trusted, that His love is constant and near.

God's love shows in the gentle hug of a friend who knows you're hurting but doesn't know why. God's love shines in the gentle touch of a nurse during a chemo treatment or in the caring voice of a doctor. It appears in the act of a neighbor who returns your trash can after it blows down the street, or in the smile of your child who says, "You're the best mommy ever." It's a card on your birthday that makes you laugh or an e-mail that arrives for no other reason than to cheer you up.

God's love is all around you. When you look for Him, He will be found. His love shines through the lives of His people.

Open my eyes, Lord, so I can see Your love shining through
the lives of those who touch my life every day. Help me to
realize that this is Your love living in Your people. Let these
little gestures of love build my trust in You. Amen.

Unappreciated yet Essential

But may the God of all grace, who called us to His eternal glory by Christ Jesus, after you have suffered a while, perfect, establish, strengthen, and settle you.

1 Peter 5:10 nkjv

The story of Leah has always intrigued me. Read Genesis 29:15-30. Leah gave so much to her husband—seven children for starters! And yet she was always second-best. Maybe she was plain or lacked a sense of humor…any number of things could have made her less appealing than her sister. Whatever the reason, Leah was not adored by her husband as her sister Rachel was. It was her grief all of her life.

And what about you? Have you ever felt second-best, unimportant, or unappreciated? Are you living in the shadow of a sibling, or worse, your spouse? Do you spend your days grieving because you have been told that you are not good enough? If so, be encouraged by the example of Leah. Even though her husband never considered her to be the best at anything, even though she lived in someone's shadow every day of her life, it was from her line of descendants that Jesus Christ came.

Leah's worth was not attributed to her looks or to the affections she could win from a man. She left a legacy of descendants that would become more than just memorable. Celebrate your identity in Him and rejoice this day!

Dear Lord, help me to find my identity and self-worth in You, not in what others think of me. Help me to be confident in who You are in me. Amen.

Waiting on the Lord

*Be still before the LORD and wait patiently for
him; do not fret when men succeed in their ways,
when they carry out their wicked schemes.*

PSALM 37:7

"But Mommy, I want it *now*," cried little Suzie as she threw a temper tantrum in the middle of the aisle. As they left the toy store together, Suzie's mom wondered where she went wrong. Ever do that? Have you wondered why your child was so impulsive and needed everything *now*?

Later that evening, Suzie's mom looked at herself in the bathroom mirror and cried…not for her daughter, but for the financial pressure. *God, why can't this be fixed now? I just want not to have to worry about where our next meal will come from!* Feeling the pressure of having no money, she was also feeling the distance of God. And she wanted it all fixed—today.

All too often we are no different from our kids screaming for toys in the middle of the store. Let's face it—waiting is not easy, especially in the "I want it now" culture we live in. But as Charles Spurgeon said, "God is too good to be unkind. He is too wise to be confused. If I cannot trace His hand, I can always trust His heart." When you seek His counsel and wait until you have clarity, you have the freedom to move with confidence, either toward something that's good for you or away from something that isn't.

Time is a commodity, and we as women have to make the most of it. If you wait patiently for God's plan to unfold, for His dream for you to be revealed, you can live and walk in the confidence of knowing He is with you every step of the way.

*O Lord, help me to wait patiently for You. Quiet my urge to rush
ahead of Your plans for my life. In Jesus' name I pray. Amen.*

What Matters Most

For where your treasure is, there your heart will be also.
Matthew 6:21

Food, alcohol, an affair, shopping, exercise, hobbies, or a job...too often, instead of looking to God and the relationships He's placed in our lives, we look to other things to fill the emptiness and ease the confusion we feel. But how well we live hinges entirely on our ability to develop healthy relationships with others.

And herein lies the secret to making every day count: focusing on what matters most—time with God and those we love. This is incredibly difficult to do in a world that values anything but intimacy with others. Wealth, beauty, fame...the decision to focus on our relationships—with God and others—is directly at odds with the things society values.

If relationships with God and others are what matter most in life, we need to ask ourselves what we're doing to strengthen these closest relationships. Often, we're so caught up in life that we inadvertently put our connections with others on autopilot, hoping that the relationships will still be intact when life settles down a bit. Because life rarely settles down, we can go weeks, months, and even years without investing time in the people we love most.

Where is your heart? Is it trapped by the human desire to store up treasure in this world? Or do you focus on people the way Jesus did when He was here on earth?

O Lord, fill me with the desire for relationship with You
and with the people I love the most. Help me to realize
that if I treasure relationship above everything else, that
is where I will put my heart and my time. Amen.

Whatever We Ask

*Now this is the confidence that we have in Him, that if
we ask anything according to His will, He hears us.*

1 JOHN 5:14 NKJV

When prayers go unanswered, many of us utter accusations to God. *I thought You cared? Why is this happening to me? Are You there?* We wonder if God even exists, let alone whether He cares. It is easy to become distressed and angry with God over this one issue—prayer.

Whether we admit it or not, we have all become angry toward God for not coming through for us the way we wanted Him to. Yet our anger is unjustified. This sounds harsh, but when we truly realize and come to understand the truth that God knows infinitely and abundantly more than we can even imagine, and that He truly does love us, we can come to accept His answer to our prayer because He truly does know best.

We cannot take 1 John 5:14 out of context. The promise that we will have whatever we ask is not a blank check. Believers cannot merely pray for anything and then get it. The context refers to prayers "according to His will." In other words, when we pray, we seek God's will in the matter. We make our requests, but we submit ourselves to God's wisdom to answer in the best way possible.

*Dear Lord, teach me what it means to pray according to
Your will. Help me to trust You, Lord, with my life and to
truly believe in my heart that Your will is bigger than mine.
"Not my will, but yours be done" (Luke 22:41). Amen.*

You Go, Girl

But encourage one another daily, as long as it is called Today,
so that none of you may be hardened by sin's deceitfulness.
HEBREWS 3:13

A word of encouragement. A pat on the back for a job well done. How do these things make you feel? What about when you get a little hand-written note in the mail that simply says thanks, or even when a friend treats you to lunch? How about the "I love you, Mom" picture?

Whenever these things happen to me, I feel as if I am on top of the world, and I believe I can accomplish anything! I love feeling appreciated. I imagine you do too!

But there's an enemy lurking around, and he has set out to steal, kill, and destroy the joy in your heart (John 10:10). Satan is the master of deceit. And he would love nothing more than to discourage you and tempt you to sin. His traps are customized to each individual, and he knows his or her vulnerabilities and areas of weakness. But the verse for today gives us the remedy to fight against Satan's scheming— encouragement. We are instructed to encourage one another so that sin cannot sabotage our hearts. Fighting Satan is not a one-person job! We definitely need one another.

My word of encouragement to you is this: Know that you are not alone and that you are loved! The Father has a beautiful plan for you and those around you. Stay strong and pass along a word of encouragement to someone today!

Dear Lord, help me to be an encouragement to others.
Open my eyes that I may see the women You bring into my
path today who need a special touch from You. Amen.

Letting Go of the Past

Forget the former things; do not dwell on the past.
ISAIAH 43:18

Finding true freedom in Christ requires letting the past be the past. But many of us aren't able to do that. Though we know intellectually that Christ has freed us, our memories continue to haunt us, and we repeatedly put ourselves down for things we did. Some things we've kept to ourselves and pray that no one ever finds out. Some things we're ashamed others may already know.

Whatever it is, whenever it was, whatever is dragging you down, now is the time to let it go. You can learn from your mistakes and be disappointed you made them in the first place, but if you want to be free, you cannot keep pointing to them as evidence of your unworthiness or failure. That's not what God wants for you.

Whatever holds us hostage keeps us from enjoying a deeper, fuller relationship with Christ. Surrendering your past is not about dwelling on the things you did. It's about putting it under the blood of Jesus and focusing on the One who looks beyond those things and into your heart.

Right here, right now, ask God for His guidance, strength, and power as you release the hold any actions or thoughts have on you. Let the past be the past. Get back to the present and concentrate solely on Him who can heal and lead you.

O Lord, let me lay down my past burdens at Your feet and leave them there. Cleanse my mind of sinful shadows and fill me with the joy of Your grace and salvation. Amen.

Life Together

They broke bread in their homes and ate
together with glad and sincere hearts.

ACTS 2:46

A few years ago, our church began to reach out to our city through a midweek ministry called Community Groups. The topics of these groups range from supportive Bible study to water aerobics! Anyone can attend. Whatever interests, hobbies, or skills people have, groups are available for them. Or they can begin groups themselves!

Many churches across our nation have begun to realize the need for strong relationships within the church and the community. We are seeing an explosion of the small-group ministry concept nationwide! I believe that life lessons are best caught and taught within a small group.

Why? Because a small group is small! It's intimate and real. In a small group, people become connected on a deeper level than they could in a corporate church gathering. They can support one another in everyday circumstances. Participants feel as if they are experiencing life the way God intended!

Did you know that Jesus was a part of a small group? During His life on earth, Jesus spent the majority of His time with His 12 disciples. He spent even more time with just three—Peter, James, and John.

You were not created to go through life alone. Life is just too hard! I encourage you today to become connected to a group of fellow believers and begin to do life together!

Dear Lord, help me realize that You did not create me
to be alone. Direct my steps and allow other believers to
come into my life who will encourage me, support me,
and most of all, help me to be more like You! Amen.

Lighting the Way

But if we walk in the light, as he is in the light, we
have fellowship with one another, and the blood
of Jesus, his Son, purifies us from all sin.

1 JOHN 1:7

It's a bright and sunny morning. I wake up to the same list of tasks I face most days: get ready, prepare breakfast for my family, feed the dogs, grab my list of things to do, get everything I need into my car...but somehow, the load seems a little lighter today, a little easier. I realize that the brilliant sky has brightened my outlook on the day. Sunshine is a wonderful thing.

Light is so powerful and extraordinary that it diffuses darkness. Without its power, we would be unable to live. Sunlight especially has the power to make plant life grow and flourish as well as add balance to the chemical structure of our own bodies. It balances the air we breathe.

So does God. The Bible says, "God is light; in him there is no darkness at all" (1 John 1:5). When it comes to living extraordinarily in this life, He is the light that keeps you balanced as you walk the path He has ordained for you. When the darkness would surround you and the enemy would try to hurt you, allow Jesus to be your light. When He lives in you, you become the light of the world. So "let your light shine before men [and women], that they may see your good deeds and praise your Father in heaven" (Matthew 5:16).

Dear Lord, thank You that You have prepared my way
and have lighted my path. Help me to remain close to You
and not give in to the darkness of this world. Amen.

Listen Up

He who answers before listening—that is his folly and his shame.
PROVERBS 18:13

Most women I know love to talk. Did you know some experts believe that each day women use three times as many words as men do? Maybe that's why women are so relational. At the heart of relationships is communication.

The art of good communication includes knowing when to speak and when to sit back and listen. There are moments in life when words are just not appropriate. When your best friend has just learned that she has cancer, when a teenager in your church finds out she is pregnant, when you or someone you know has lost a loved one in an unexpected way…these are times when words just don't seem to fit. Your gentle presence and a listening ear speak volumes.

Being a good listener is a beautiful character trait to possess. "Everyone should be quick to listen, slow to speak and slow to become angry" (James 1:19). When you take the time to truly listen to someone, putting aside all thoughts about your response, you will gain a very clear understanding of her life. You will be in a position to offer her the best possible help—a shoulder to lean on and someone to trust.

Dear Lord, help me to be quick to listen. Attune my ears to those hurting around me. May I be a vessel of comfort to be used by You. Amen.

Live Lovingly

Be imitators of God, therefore, as dearly loved children
and live a life of love, just as Christ loved us and gave him-
self up for us as a fragrant offering and sacrifice to God.

EPHESIANS 5:1-2

What a beautiful passage of Scripture! I am reminded about every-thing that Christ went through on the cross for me and for you. What love! He loved you so much that He became a living sacrifice, giving up His life to save you.

I want that kind of deep and immense love to exist in me. Do you? The good news is that when you become a Christian and Christ lives in you, His love becomes a part of who you are. However, showing that love to others is our responsibility.

When you demonstrate God's love to others, you are being an imi-tation of Him. As you choose to imitate God through giving to others, you will receive the greatest blessing of all. Always be "remembering the words the Lord Jesus himself said: 'It is more blessed to give than to receive'" (Acts 20:35).

Seek out ways in which you can give to others. Be an imitator of Christ and live lovingly today!

Dear Lord, thank You for loving me. Help me to be a model of Your
love to others today. Help me to be an imitator of You! Amen.

Longings Fulfilled

If anyone acknowledges that Jesus is the Son of God,
God lives in him and he in God. And so we know
and rely on the love God has for us. God is love. Who-
ever lives in love lives in God, and God in him.

1 JOHN 4:15-16

To love and be loved—it's what we were made for. As little girls, we longed for the attention of our fathers. As young women, we longed for the attention of the boys we hung around. Then *he* comes along—the love of our life.

But strangely, this longing in our hearts to be loved continues in life and will continue until we find rest and fulfillment in the ultimate love of God. Human, finite love can't fill the void. Learning to understand, accept, and embrace God's infinite love is the only way to become truly satisfied.

Everything God does is infused with love. His love for you knows no bounds. You can rest in knowing that He is ultimately the only One who can fill your longings and be your heart's desire. Ask Him today to show you His love. And be expecting to find it even in the most unsuspecting places.

O Giver of Love, fill my heart with Your love. Enfold me
with Your everlasting and ever-loving arms. Let Your
love for me calm my longing to be loved. Amen.

Love Is a Verb

Dear children, let us not love with words or
tongue but with actions and in truth.

1 John 3:18

I love to hear my husband or children say, "I love you." I loved to hear my dad tell me he loved me too! It made me feel special.

I also feel loved because their words are accompanied by kind actions. My son may give me a hug or help me with the groceries, my daughter might do the laundry, my husband takes care of my car and works hard to provide for our needs. They do not use just their words to show their love. They live out their love!

God desires the same of you. He wants you to show your love for Him and for others by your actions. Saying that you love God is easy, proving it is another thing.

Love is a verb—an action. It might include spending time with Him, taking a meal to a sick church member, cleaning an elderly woman's home, or serving food to the homeless at a local shelter. All these things touch the heart of God. He is pleased when you prove your love through action. So find a way today to show your love for Him!

Dear Lord, help me to remember to act out my love. I
want to show the world Your love, not only by what I
say but also by what I do. I love You, Lord. Amen.

Love's Identity Crisis

[Love] always protects, always trusts,
always hopes, always perseveres.

1 CORINTHIANS 13:7

Do you know that the Sanskrit language has ninety-six words for love? The ancient Persian language has eighty words, and the Greek language has four. Can you think of some English synonyms for *love*?

It is no wonder our culture has this whole "love" thing mixed up. Posted all over the headlines are stories of actors, actresses, athletes, and singers falling in and out of love week after week.

With only one word to describe love, Americans are confused. Relationships fail as people simply fall out of love. Many report not feeling the same way they once did. Their passion runs dry.

As I look back on my relationship with God, I cannot help but reflect on the times I have been unlovable. Yet through those times God chose to love me and stick with me, encouraging me through my good days and my bad days. To love truly is to love others when they are unlovable, to persevere regardless of what you may be feeling toward them. Kids and husbands included.

God calls us to display His love to others. Put your own feelings aside and persevere with somebody. Show her the same love that God has shown to you.

Love is a decision. God's dream for you is that you would choose to love!

Dear Lord, in gratefulness for Your love to me, help me to love others more deeply, more consistently, more unselfishly. Let Your love shine through me in every aspect of my life. Amen.

Majestic Love

*How great is the love the Father has lavished on
us, that we should be called children of God!*
1 John 3:1

Living out God's dream means you know His love. But how does
that happen?

Just before my dad died, he took my hand and told me how much
he loved me. In that moment I was a little girl all over again. Amazingly,
God's love for you is greater than what my dad communicated in that
magical moment. When you know of God's love, everything changes.

Paul wants you "to grasp how wide and long and high and deep
is the love of Christ, and to know this love that surpasses knowledge"
(Ephesians 3:18-19). God's love reaches to every area of our lives. It's a
love that never ends. He has adopted us as daughters and has invited
us to know a love that's beyond our wildest imagination. John takes
us further and tells us to "know and rely on the love God has for us"
(1 John 4:16).

How about you? How do you experience His love? Through the
smell of fresh cut grass or the ambience of the setting sun? Maybe
you're blessed by an answered prayer, or maybe you have had to rely
on Him to make a tough choice in a difficult circumstance.

Pray that God will remove any barriers that keep you from relying
on His perfect, beautiful, unfailing love. Experience it to the full, and
rely on it instead of your own fears. When you experience this kind
of love you can truly exclaim with John, "How great is the love the
Father has lavished on us!"

*Father, thank You for loving me so lavishly. Help me to fully
bask in Your love. Break down the barriers that keep me
from knowing and relying on Your love for me. Amen.*

Making the Grade

*Test me, O LORD, and try me, examine my heart
and my mind; for your love is ever before me,
and I walk continually in your truth.*

PSALM 26:2-3

I have never really enjoyed taking tests. When I was a teacher, administering tests to my students never bothered me. But when it comes to *taking* a test...yikes!

David was a pretty bold guy to ask God for a test! He wanted God to examine his life, inside and out, to make sure that he was living a life pleasing to Him.

David was not perfect, but he definitely made the grade. "I have found David son of Jesse a man after my own heart; he will do everything I want him to do" (Acts 13:22). To be described as a "man after God's heart" is something pretty special!

Have you ever asked God to test you? To examine your life and grade you on your performance? It's a scary concept to think about. You can always test yourself as well. Do some research and find out what others think about you. Read your Bible and ask God to reveal areas of your life that need attention. Work on those areas. Seek to follow Him and make Him first in your life. If you do, you should pass every test with flying colors!

Dear Lord, I want to live a life that is pleasing to You. I want to make You first in my life, walking continually in Your truth. Help me to have the strength I need to do what You have called me to do. Amen.

Measureless Love

For I am persuaded that neither death nor life, nor angels nor principalities nor powers, nor things present nor things to come, nor height nor depth, nor any other created thing, shall be able to separate us from the love of God which is in Christ Jesus our Lord.

ROMANS 8:38-39 NKJV

As women, we are believed to be more relational than men. We tend to have an innate ability to connect with others in a way that is different from our male counterparts. Not better, just different. Being more relational also means we can be more emotional. For example, developing a relationship may be easier for us, but letting it go is harder. And sometimes we do need to let go.

Separation is difficult. Whether it be separation from a friend due to relocation, separation from a child who leaves for college, or even separation from a spouse, in any case, it hurts! That's why I love today's Scripture, which says that nothing will be able to separate us from God's love. You can never be hurt or disappointed by God. His love never fails! People will let you down because humans are not perfect. God will never let you down because He *is* perfect!

God's love cannot be measured because it has no bounds. It is unending and a part of who you are as a believer. It is a relationship that will never have cause for separation. Rejoice, my sister, that there is a friend who sticks closer than a brother (Proverbs 18:24). That's a relationship that will not fail!

Dear Lord, thank You for Your unending love for me. I am so glad to know that I do not need to earn Your love...it is just there. Thank You for the relationship I have with You. Amen.

My Neat, Tidy Box

Oh, the depth of the riches both of the wisdom and knowledge of God! How unsearchable are His judgments and His ways past finding out!

ROMANS 11:33 NKJV

I love my world to be ordered, in control, and predictable. And I like having everyone follow the rules and do things the way I have laid them out. If only it was that easy! If only our world would cooperate with us and fit into our neat, tidy box, life would pass by much more smoothly. Don't you agree?!

But this kind of existence has a downside. Living such a life stifles our ability to be stretched and to grow in spiritual maturity. By staying in our comfort zones, we never learn to trust God during times of uncertainty and difficulty.

God's Word tells us that His ways are higher than ours. His knowledge and wisdom are far greater than ours. He can see the whole purpose behind the things that happen in our lives. When life is not the way it's supposed to be, our vision is much more limited. It only makes sense to trust the One who can see the situation from every angle and who we know has our best interest in mind as He unveils His dream for our lives.

O Lord of all knowledge and wisdom, give me a heart that will yield to Your way, for the path of life that You have chosen for me is perfect. Help me to embrace the adventure of following You and to enjoy a life that far exceeds anything I will find in my neat tidy box. Amen.

My Way Versus His Way

*"For my thoughts are not your thoughts, neither
are your ways my ways," declares the* LORD.

ISAIAH 55:8

Husbands! Ugh! Sometimes he just doesn't get it. And after a few years together, I've learned that sometimes I have missed his point too. I can get so focused on my way of doing things that to do anything different seems...well, ridiculous!

If we're not careful, our relationship with God can become this way. A sort of tug-of-war between our flesh and His perfect wisdom.

God sees the big picture. He sees the beginning, the end, and everything between. He knows you and His plan for your life intimately. His way is perfect, divine, flawless.

God wants you to follow His lead. Solomon understood this: "Lean not on your own understanding; in all your ways acknowledge him, and he will make your paths straight" (Proverbs 3:5-6). Remember, you are praying to an infinite, perfect God, who is more loving and wise than any human on this earth. Just let go and let God's way become yours!

*Dear Lord, I pray that I will yield to Your loving dream
for my life and learn to live in Your perfect plan for
me. Give me patience as I wait for You to answer my
prayers in Your most perfect way and time. Amen.*

Necessary Change

For the word of the LORD is right and true; he is faithful in all he does. The LORD loves righteousness and justice; the earth is full of his unfailing love.

PSALM 33:4-5

I love the classic movie *Anne of Green Gables*. One of my favorite lines from Anne is, "Tomorrow is a brand-new day with no mistakes in it!"

One of the best things about life is that tomorrow doesn't have to be the same as today. You can learn new habits, get rid of unwanted old ones, and do something to improve your life.

You can be secure that Christ's love for you is unchanging. That assurance allows you the freedom to make needed changes in your own life. Knowing that God really loves you includes understanding that He wants the best for you and is willing to help you get it. He will help and support you through the choices and changes you need to make. He will be with you all the way. James 1:5 says that if we lack wisdom, we can go to Him, and He will guide us.

Take a minute for personal reflection. Though God's love is unchanging, how do you need to change in order to more fully embrace His love and friendship? Do you need to accept yourself before you can accept God's love more fully? Do you need to forgive yourself and others before you bathe in His love? Do you need to trust your heavenly Father more?

Take your needs to Him in prayer. Yearn to be more like Him. Allow His unchanging love to change you!

Dear Lord, I need You to give me the courage to face my shortcomings. Give me the strength to take the first step in changing my ways. I want to let the power of the Holy Spirit fill me and change my life. Amen.

No Credit Card Required

How priceless is your unfailing love!
PSALM 36:7

We live in a time when everything we do has a price. Movies, amusement parks, parking…everything costs money.

Ironically, the one thing we possess that is worth more than everything else, we receive for no price whatsoever—God's love. Our Father sent His one and only Son to die for our sins once and for all (Hebrews 7:27) because He loves us. There is nothing you need to do for God to love you. He loved you from the very beginning.

This week, take your family to a beautiful landscape—away from the craziness of the world. Drive to the mountains. Sit by a lake or river. Stand in the middle of an open field at night staring into the sky. Meditate for a moment on God's faithfulness, righteousness, and love, and consider His dream for your life. Talk to Him about your life. Get together with a friend, your husband, or children and talk about God's love in your lives. Thank God and give praise to Him for His many blessings. These moments, and God's love, are priceless!

O loving Father, thank You for the priceless and unmatchable gift of Your Son. Thank You for the myriads of blessings You have showered on my life through Your love. I am Your grateful and loving daughter, and I adore You. Amen.

Not Part of the Plan

A perverse man stirs up dissension, and
a gossip separates close friends.

PROVERBS 16:28

Gossip has no place in the life God has in mind for us. It's a dangerous spark that sneaks into our conversations as seemingly innocent facts or as something to pray about. Never is it helpful and uplifting.

The Bible says that a gossip betrays confidence and causes quarrels (Proverbs 20:19; 26:20). Like a spark on dry timber, the words of a gossip can create a firestorm that destroys friendships, relationships, and reputations.

As Christians, we need to use our time and words more wisely. Don't listen to or spread rumors and half-truths. We must have the courage to stop gossip before it starts, even if that means gently rebuking a friend.

"Whatever is true, whatever is noble, whatever is right, whatever is pure, whatever is lovely, whatever is admirable—if anything is excellent or praiseworthy—think about such things" (Philippians 4:8).

Train yourself not to listen to or pass along gossip, for the consequences are far too hurtful. Use only words that are encouraging, uplifting, and edifying to the soul! If you can't say something good about someone, don't say anything!

O Lord, help me to resist the desire to be a gossip or to listen
to such talk. Guide me in Your perfect way. Fill my life and
mouth with words that are honorable and full of praise
for You and others. In Christ's name I pray. Amen.

Nothing Hidden, Nothing Held Back

*For godly sorrow produces repentance leading to salvation, not
to be regretted; but the sorrow of the world produces death.*

2 Corinthians 7:10 nkjv

There is a difference between being sorry and truly repenting, which
includes having a change of heart and direction. Repentance begins
with recognizing our sin. Though we will always struggle with sin
(Romans 7:15-20), repentance allows us to restore our relationship
with God. Genuine repentance occurs only when we accept responsibility for our wrong actions and confess them. Nothing hidden,
nothing held back.

David knew that true repentance goes beyond sacrifices and burnt
offerings. "The sacrifices of God are a broken spirit; a broken and
a contrite heart—these, O God, You will not despise" (Psalm 51:17).

Sins you cover, God will uncover. Sins you uncover, God will cover.
When God reveals a sin to you, repent. Ask forgiveness. Change your
ways. The result will be joy, gladness, and a purified heart. You'll enjoy
an unhindered relationship with Him! And you'll be free.

*O God, hear my cry for forgiveness. I come to You with a broken
spirit and a contrite heart, for I know how badly I have sinned
against You. Restore my life with joy and gladness. Renew my
heart so I can have a close relationship with You. Amen.*

On His Hands

I will not forget you! See, I have engraved
you on the palms of my hands.

Isaiah 49:15-16

Hands are an interesting addition to the body. They come in all different shapes, sizes, and even colors. There are young hands and old hands. Smooth hands and wrinkled hands. Callused hands and bony hands. They are used for picking things up, for cleaning (yes, the *C* word), for cooking, and for comfort. Hands can also have many misuses as well, as in cases of abuse and violence.

When we look to Jesus, His hands always bring about good. In His ministry on earth, Jesus used His hands to heal the sick. To comfort those who needed comforting. To work in His father's carpentry shop. To hold and teach children. To confront sin and flip tables in the temple.

But that's not all. The Word says that we've been engraved on God's precious hands! And in the engraving process, the desired figure or artwork is burned into the product in order to make a lasting impression that cannot be removed. He remembers you—always!

You are not just *in* His hands; you are *on* His hands! We so often hear that we are *in* His hands, but today, claim His promise that you cannot be removed!

Dear Lord, thank You for dying for me on the cross. Thank You
that I can have salvation by believing in You. I am so happy
to know that I am forever on *Your hands and not just* in *Your*
hands. Use my hands today to direct someone to You! Amen.

Pick Me...Pick Me!

Serve the LORD with gladness.
PSALM 100:2 NKJV

Have you ever been at an event and wanted so badly to be chosen to participate? You know, you are so excited that you wave your hand like a hummingbird's wings just so someone would see you, yelling "Pick me! Pick me!"

I believe that God wants that kind of heart in us, that kind of desire to serve Him. He wants us to be willing to go where He sends us and to do what He has planned for us regardless of the cost. Volunteers do not have to be pressured into service—they just serve!

The body of Christ offers so many ways to serve. From taking a meal to someone who is sick, to staying after the church service to stack chairs, opportunities to serve are all around us. When we serve others, we serve Christ! Jesus tells us, "I tell you the truth, whatever you did for one of the least of these brothers of mine, you did for me" (Matthew 25:40). Approach God with the heart of a volunteer today, and be willing to serve. You *will* be blessed and you *will* be picked!

Dear Lord, help me not to fall into the trap of serving only me. Help me to put aside the cultural lie that I must look out only for myself. Give me an opportunity to show Your love to someone today! Amen.

Picture This

*Anyone who listens to the word but does not do what it says is
like a man who looks at his face in a mirror and, after looking at
himself, goes away and immediately forgets what he looks like.*

JAMES 1:23-24

I love pictures! Have you ever wondered who invented the camera?
Many believe George Eastman invented the roll-film camera in 1888.
But actually, somebody else made the camera first. The first camera
that was small and portable enough to be practical for photography
was built by Johann Zahn in 1685.

Pictures allow us to capture moments in time, to make memories
that last forever. And with the technology available today, we can have
these keepsakes in seconds!

When it comes to memorizing Scripture, a picture captured in
the mind, never to be erased, would be wonderful! James says that
anyone who "looks intently into the perfect law that gives freedom,
and continues to do this, not forgetting what he has heard, but doing
it—he will be blessed in what he does" (James 1:25).

Do you want freedom? Do you want to be blessed? Study the Bible.
Find a way to memorize Scripture and obey it. Don't just walk away
from hearing God's Word at church or at a conference and forget
what you learned. Write it down. Use your mind like a camera and
take a "picture" of God's spoken promises that you can reflect on for
years to come!

*Dear Lord, help me remember Your Word. Help me
learn how to memorize Scripture. I want to reflect
on Your promises to me all of my life. Amen.*

Praise to the King

Let everything that has breath praise the LORD.

PSALM 150:6

Praise songs have always been my favorites. I listen to praise music most of the time when I'm in the car with the kids, running errands, going to church, or going to a meeting. When I'm alone, I give it all I've got, and I often wonder why I didn't hit the big time. But my kids quickly remind me why! In a lot of ways the Bible is a book of praise to God. Check out any concordance, and you'll realize how often the writers mention praising the Lord.

Have you noticed that singing is easy when everything is going right? Singing God's praises when things aren't going well is a discipline. It may take effort, but I promise you that it will change your attitude and help you see God's dream for you unfolding even in the not-so-good times. Martin Luther once said, "As long as believers praise and thank God, then temptation, sadness, and unbelief disappear."

Your God is the Almighty King. He cares for you. He loves you. He protects you. He saved you. He has big plans for you. That's something to praise Him for. Your God is awesome. He is worthy of your praise regardless of what is happening in your life. So sing and praise His name!

God keeps me singing. I hope you have a song in your heart too!

My Almighty King, let me sing Your praises throughout the day. Let me sing when things are going smoothly and I see dreams unfolding. Let me sing when things are in shambles, so my sadness will disappear. Amen.

Pray for Rain

Be patient, then, brothers [or sisters], until the Lord's coming.
See how the farmer waits for the land to yield its valuable crop
and how patient he is for the autumn and spring rains. You too,
be patient and stand firm, because the Lord's coming is near.

JAMES 5:7-8

"Rain, rain, go away, come again another day!" Remember that silly song from childhood? It was so important to us as children because when it rained, we couldn't go outside to play. The funny thing is, I still find myself singing that song as a mother.

The fact is, rain has monumental benefits to the growth and maintenance of the earth and its atmosphere. Rain refreshes plant life and causes it to flourish. It causes crops to grow and trees to produce fruit. I imagine that it does take a great deal of patience for the farmer in our passage of Scripture to wait for that much-needed rainfall!

Just as patience is tested in the waiting farmer, patience continues to be tested when the rain comes. Rain often challenges our plans for the day—the picnic is postponed, or the ball game is canceled.

In either case, patience is a virtue that you must possess. Patience produces perseverance in your life—perseverance to keep on living for God and serving Him. The Lord's return is drawing nearer each day. With each rain that falls (or doesn't fall), may you be reminded that the King is coming. Stand firm and wait on Him!

Dear Lord, I want to be a patient person. Help me to trust in You
and have perseverance until Your coming. Bring on the rain! Amen.

Prayer at Its Best

*The earnest prayer of a righteous person has
great power and wonderful results.*

JAMES 5:16 NLT

Too often our prayers turn into pleaful monologues. We present nothing more than our requests to Him, only our worries and concerns about life and maybe a thanks every once in a while. But intimacy is about seeing into another person, and you can only see into somebody else by listening to what he or she has to say—a two-way conversation of give-and-take, talking and listening. Prayer at its best is an intimate conversation between you and God.

When we really listen, we're better able to hear God speaking to us by His Spirit, through the Bible, through friends, through circumstances, or through a gentle "knowing" that settles in our hearts. When He responds, we know His words will draw us closer to Him because whatever He asks of us is a reflection of His character. When we do more of what He wants, we become more like Him.

Slowing down to pray is difficult in our time-starved society, but we must do it. Getting alone and being still before God in prayer reinforces our dependence on Him and increases our intimacy with Him.

Pray specifically. Then listen. God will respond.

*Draw me near, Lord, as I come to You to pray. Fill
me with Your presence and heart. Let me hear from
You and know Your will for my life. Amen.*

Praying God's Will in Difficult Times

Lord, teach us to pray.

LUKE 11:1

When my life feels out of control, I want peace! A place to get away from everything and just be alone. I will often pray, *Lord, get me out of this mess—now!*

When life circumstances seem chaotic and hopeless, it's easy to pray according to our will, not God's. We want relief, escape, freedom, less pain. When life is difficult, we can feel confused and have trouble finding our way. Have you ever thought, *God, are You even there? Do You hear me? Are You on vacation?*

Even if you are still waiting for God to answer your prayers, you can know that God is *not* on vacation. He hears you loud and clear. Maybe it's time to reevaluate what you are asking for. Instead of praying for what *you* may think is best, begin praying for what *God* thinks is best. If you don't know, ask Him to show you.

Praying for God's will during difficult times is scary. Sometimes, His will may be that you continue in this difficult season for a while. However, always remember that He is shaping and molding you into a stronger, more mature woman. An extraordinary woman!

Lord, teach me how to pray so that my prayers reflect Your will for my life. Give me patience to humbly wait for Your guiding hand. Amen.

Precious in His Sight

*Since you were precious in My sight, you have
been honored, and I have loved you.*

ISAIAH 43:4 NKJV

When I was growing up, my dad always called me his little angel. I was beautiful in his eyes, and that made me feel special. Over the years, I've grown to understand how much my heavenly Father loves me. He loves far more deeply than my earthly father ever could. All of us are precious in His sight. Sometimes that's hard for us to believe. Maybe you're even thinking, *There's nothing special about me.* But you are. Everything about you is special and precious. You are beautiful in His eyes because He created you a certain way, with matchless abilities and special gifts.

If you've become lost along the way, and if you cannot hear your Father's voice encouraging you, now is the time to listen again. Rediscover the qualities God placed in you before you came into being. Those are the special qualities God wants you to use so you can live out His dream for your life!

*O Lord, let me see myself as You see me: beautifully made in
Your image with unique and special gifts. Help me to feel the
depth of Your love for me, even if I have tarnished memories
of a father's love. Fill me with delight and joy as I eagerly
await the unfolding dream You have for my life. Amen.*

Purpose of Waiting

Wait for the LORD; be strong and take
heart and wait for the LORD.

PSALM 27:14

Waiting is hard! We don't enjoy waiting for traffic, long lines at the store, the last family member to get in the car, test results, or answers to our prayers. Even when things are going well in our lives, we hate waiting for the next positive moment to happen.

But waiting is part of God's plan. God has many reasons to let us wait, none of which we see until after the fact. For instance, God may want us to wait until we gain more knowledge, more favorable circumstances arise, we have the support of others, financial provision is available, or we are emotionally prepared.

Often we don't even know why we are waiting. But God does.

He is an all-knowing God. He knows when you sit and when you rise; He perceives your thoughts from afar. He discerns your going out and your lying down. He is familiar with all your ways. He knows the purpose for any waiting in your life. Your job is to trust Him. You can either wait patiently and learn what you can in the process or wait impatiently and miss whatever refinement the delay holds for you.

Pray as you wait. As you do, you'll discover the value of letting things come in God's time. You'll also find the beauty in waiting—the possibility that God's dream for your life is just on the other side.

All-knowing God, I don't like waiting; it makes me nervous.
Calm me with Your Spirit that I may learn what I can in the
waiting. Give me confidence that You are in control so I will
rest and wait patiently for Your guiding hand. Amen.

Questioning God

I will question you, and you shall answer me.

JOB 38:3

When you face seemingly insurmountable problems, such as your child's diabetes, your parent's pancreatic cancer, or your own lost eyesight, is God's presence in your life enough?

Few people in all of human history have suffered to the extent Job did. He cried out, but God did not answer, at least not directly. Instead, God revealed His sovereignty over all creation, including Job's life. God did not explain Job's suffering.

Your love for God cannot be conditioned on the way you think He is treating you. Or on the way you think He *should* treat you. Perseverance through great suffering is an indication of your trust in God. Faith in God must be maintained through times of trial as well as times of blessing. Regardless of what you face in life, you can trust that God is in control. You must rely on Him and His goodness.

Read Job 38. Answer the questions God asks of Job. In the midst of your next trial, go back and answer those same questions.

The answer is God. Everything points back to Him! His presence is all you need!

*O sovereign Lord, when trials come my way, help me
to persevere in faith, confident that You have my life in
the palm of Your hand and that no harm will befall me
without Your awareness and direction. Amen.*

Reflections

Your works are wonderful.

PSALM 139:14

Yosemite National Park features the most beautiful and tranquil lake I have ever seen—Mirror Lake. Sometimes it sits so perfectly still that you can see your complete reflection just as if you were looking straight into a mirror. It is perhaps one of God's most beautiful creations.

Yet you may be thinking, *That doesn't sound like a great lake to me. I don't enjoy looking at myself in a mirror at all.* For some, it's a real struggle to get up each morning to get ready for the day, knowing that there is going to be a mirror above the sink.

What do you see when you view your reflection in your mirror? Psalm 139 says the reflection in the mirror you see every morning is fearfully and wonderfully made. Verse 16 says, "Your eyes saw my unformed body. All the days ordained for me were written in your book before one of them came to be." We are created by God, and all of our days were planned and dreamed out before we were even born! That very God sees you today, with all of your messy hair and with no makeup. And still He knows you're beautiful. Ask Him to help you to look into that mirror and see the reflection that He sees—the precious, extraordinary woman He planned for you to be.

Dear Lord, help me to see myself in the way You do.
May I be a reflection of Your beauty and grace so that
others will desire to know more about You. Amen.

Resolving to Get It Done

*For a righteous man may fall seven times and rise
again, but the wicked shall fall by calamity.*

Proverbs 24:16 NJKV

When Megan was a young girl, Tim taught her how to ride a bike. Megan was so afraid, yet she worked so hard to learn. Finally the day came when she was ready to ride alone—with no help! She pedaled and pedaled just like a pro! But then, suddenly, fear came over her face, and then panic. She froze! Tim sprinted after her, but he was too late. She was already lying in the briar bush! He scooped her up in his arms and wondered if she would ever ride again. Of course, she did.

Failure is never final until a person quits trying. As the person continues to try, failure is really no more than a setback—a possibility to learn from mistakes and try again. Righteous people may fail time and time again, but they continue to rise again, to get up and keep trying.

Failure is a part of the human experience. It can be painful and embarrassing, but it can also be your greatest teacher. God's definition of success does not preclude failure. But it includes a willingness to refuse to quit, to learn from one's mistakes, to try again.

Whatever you have resolved to do—lose weight, exercise more, have devotions each day, take a class, have time alone with your man—don't quit! Resolve to stay with it.

With God all things are possible. Get started and make it happen!

*Dear Lord, help me to understand that failure is part of
life, part of the process of learning and becoming better.
Give me strength to face the failures that will come my way.
Give me courage to rise up and start again. Amen.*

Leave Them in Your Stilettos

The eternal God is your refuge, and underneath are the everlasting arms.

DEUTERONOMY 33:27

It's the end of the day. You've been running around as usual. Maybe you've put in a full day at work, cared for the kids, cleaned, cooked, driven the carpool, and bought groceries at the store. In any case, all is done, and it's time to settle in for the night. What's the first thing you do? I know what I do—I take off my shoes! My feet are usually the first area of my body that screams for help. When my shoes are off, I feel like a new woman.

Don't you wish you could let go of your cares and worries as easily as you can take off your shoes? Wouldn't you enjoy laying down anxieties, releasing troubles, and forgetting your pain so effortlessly?

Unfortunately, it's not that easy. However, God does promise several times in His Word that He will provide strength when you need it most. "They remembered that God was their Rock, that God Most High was their Redeemer" (Psalm 78:35). He is your strength. He is your place of refuge, as today's verse reminds us. But you must be willing to let go. You must be willing to surrender everything to Him and to press in close to Him.

So when you come to the end of your day, know that He is all you need! Regardless of which way the wind blows, you can trust God with your problems. Close the closet door and prayerfully leave them in your stilettos!

Dear Lord, help me to give up and let You take control of my life today. I am choosing to rest in Your promise that You are my place of refuge. I delight in You and thank You for loving me. Amen.

Send Me

Then I heard the voice of the Lord saying, "Whom shall I send?
And who will go for us?" And I said, "Here am I. Send me!"

ISAIAH 6:8

Isaiah proclaimed his wonderful prophecies of the coming Messiah and King during treacherous and dangerous times. The nations around Judah were conspiring to invade. They were plotting the ruin of the nation. So when Isaiah was called by God to be His spokesperson, he was accepting a daunting and dangerous assignment. Yet Isaiah accepted it willingly and confidently.

God calls you to stand for Him too. Probably the greatest deterrent to an effective ministry is the belief that everything in your life has to be perfect before you can serve Him. Too often as women we think that we need to be highly educated and flawless in a million different ways to handle what God lays before us. But being willing to serve is all that's needed—God will provide the rest. Just as God provided for great leaders in the Old Testament who thought they were weak, lacked skill, or were insignificant, so too will He provide the talents you need. For Moses, who thought he was not an eloquent speaker, God provided the words (Exodus 4:10-12). For Gideon, who considered himself insignificant, God provided confidence (Judges 6:15-16). For Esther, who was one of many women in a pagan king's court, God provided the wisdom and strength to plead for her people (Esther 4:12-16). Serving the Lord in the most significant way begins with an open and willing heart.

Open your heart to the Lord. God's calling on your life will never lack God's supply.

Dear Lord, give me a willing heart to serve You
and do great things in Your name. Amen.

Shared Comfort

*Praise be to the God and Father of our Lord Jesus Christ, the
Father of compassion and the God of all comfort, who comforts us in all our troubles, so that we can comfort those in any
trouble with the comfort we ourselves have received from God.*

2 CORINTHIANS 1:3-4

The loss of a loved one, cancer, kids growing up and moving out,
job loss, marital difficulties…you name it, whether it's your wound
or someone's you love, God won't waste it. He'll work in it to reveal
Himself, to show that He can be trusted, that He is faithful and
loving. He is there to comfort us. Through our wounds, we learn to
love more deeply and empathize more carefully.

God comforts us so that we may more effectively share His comfort
with others. What a glorious picture of the body of believers lifting
one another up in difficult times! When facing life's trials, trust that
God is looking out for you, empathizing with you, loving you, and
holding you in His arms. Then take the compassion He shows you
and pay it forward to those suffering around you.

*Dear God of all comfort, when I am hurting, send Your comfort to
surround me. When others need my care, fill me with comfort so I
am ready and willing to share Your comfort with them. Amen.*

Sheltering Cove

*He who dwells in the shelter of the Most High
will rest in the shadow of the Almighty.*

PSALM 91:1

Imagine you are on a mini-vacation. Picture yourself sitting on a beautiful white sandy beach with the warm sun shining down on you and the crystal clear blue ocean waves lapping slowly into the small secluded cove you have discovered. You dip your toes into the sea and feel the perfect temperature of the water. All is right with the world, and you are feeling sheltered completely from the busyness and trials of life.

Now, remember that warm and fuzzy feeling and reread the key verse for today. Dwelling in the shelter of the Most High is a lot like enjoying the shelter of your little cove. At any time of the day, we have the opportunity to commune with a loving God, who can provide us with the shelter we need from anything we face. We can commune with Him through prayer and also through Bible reading. The book of Psalms is filled with "sheltering" verses!

I encourage you to rest in the shadow of your almighty Savior. Spend time with Him, commune with Him, and allow Him to be your cove of shelter today!

*Dear Lord, thank You that I can be at peace, knowing
that You are my shelter. Help me to rest. Help me to
make time for communion with You daily! Amen.*

Sing a New Song

*I will give thanks to the LORD because of his righteousness
and will sing praise to the name of the LORD Most High.*

PSALM 7:17

Remember the acclaimed classic *The Sound of Music,* with the lovely Julie Andrews as the governess for the spunky and energetic von Trapp children? To this day, the musical line of do-re-mi-fa-so-la-ti-do is used in music classes all over the world, yet I have never heard it sung more beautifully than by "Maria." She had the ability to turn life around for the von Trapp family through song. Her love for life and the beauty of creation always brought out the best in others. What a great movie!

Never fear—you don't need a voice like Julie Andrews to sing praise to our God. However, God does rejoice when we sing to Him. He delights in the praises of His people. One definition of worship is this: responding to all that God is with all that we are. Read that again. Are you responding with all that you are to your heavenly Father, who created your inmost being? Give yourself permission today to worship God through singing—in your car, in the shower...who cares? Sing like never before! I promise, His heart will be blessed with the sound of your music!

*Dear Lord, I sing praise to Your name today and worship
You through song. You are the wonderful Creator of
everything and deserve my praise. Help me to put aside
my fears and sing a new song of praise today! Amen.*

Sleep

*I will both lie down and sleep in peace, for you
alone, O LORD, make me dwell in safety.*

PSALM 4:8

Sleep. Need more of it? I do.

Sleep may be the most important component of renewing our
bodies every day. When was the last time you had a solid eight hours
of sleep? The pains and pressures of life sneak into our bedrooms in
the wee hours of the night. Our fast-paced lifestyle has robbed us of
sleep as we overexert ourselves trying to take care of our children,
husbands, homes, and work. The result is that we get more run down,
more anxious, and more stressed.

God's dream for your life comes alive when you are rested. When
you are focused, calm, and ready to go, you are also more confident
in God.

Are you getting the recovery time you need physically? Try resting
in Him spiritually. End each day by meditating on a special verse of
comfort. Listen to a soothing worship song. Look through a picture
album full of special memories, and thank God for them. These are
ways to quiet your heart, renew your mind, and unwind from the
day. After all, God is in total control of everything that happens to
you. Rest in the knowledge that He will safely care for you and your
needs!

Sweet dreams…

*Dear Lord, bless me with the gift of restful sleep. Calm my mind
and soothe my troubled heart. Give me peace to relax and fall
asleep, knowing You are in control of every part of my life. Amen.*

Something Beautiful

Arise, go to Zarephath...See, I have commanded a widow there to provide for you.

1 Kings 17:9

The ministry of Extraordinary Women was born out of the belief that God can do extraordinary things using ordinary women. The widow of Zarephath is no exception. In the midst of the various trials and heartaches of losing her husband and then nearly losing her son and her own life, this ordinary woman continued to trust and believe even when it seemed useless to do so.

God chose the most unlikely candidate to provide for Elijah. She could barely provide for herself. Yet she did not question God's plan. She kept on working, doing all she could with her meager supplies. God provided for the widow, her son, and His prophet Elijah.

Have you ever looked into an empty cupboard, wondering where the next meal would come from? Or maybe it's not a financial concern. Maybe your heart is an empty cupboard filled with unmet needs and extreme worries. I pray today that your hope would be found in the God who always comes through. The God who transforms the ordinary into the extraordinary, something plain into something beautiful. Allow Him to make a difference through you today!

Dear Lord, thank You for coming to my aid. When my cupboards are empty and my fuel tank is low, I pray You will fill me with the physical, emotional, and spiritual nutrients I need. Give me the divine strength to move from the ordinary to the extraordinary. Amen.

Sparkling like Gold

When He has tested me, I will come forth as gold.

Job 23:10

Job is one of the most fascinating and well-known men in the Bible. He lost his children, his vast wealth, and eventually his health. He was left with only an embittered wife and unwise friends. Can you imagine?

Yet Job knew he was not alone. He knew that God knew who he was, where he was, and what pain he was experiencing. He was given no reason for the calamity that so swiftly struck his life. Yet he did not question or turn away. He simply and resolutely chose to keep his faith in God.

Job knew God and trusted Him. Can you say the same today? It seems that nearly every day I hear of another catastrophe that has fallen on someone's life. War, hurricanes, fires, car accidents, miscarriages... when you are faced with such a tragedy, can you face it as Job did? Cry out in the midst of your sorrow to God. Know Him and trust Him.

I pray today that you will grow to know and trust your God more deeply and more resolutely than ever before. Remember the words of Job in those dark times: "He knows the way that I take; when He has tested me, I shall come forth as gold."

Dear Lord, I pray that I can face suffering the way Job did—by remaining faithful and trusting You. Thank You for Your constant care and protection over me. Make me more like You! Amen.

Spending Your Time

*Relish life with the spouse you love each and every day of your
precarious life. Each day is God's gift. It's all you get in exchange
for the hard work of staying alive. Make the most of each one!*

ECCLESIASTES 9:9 MSG

Living God's dream means living in close relationships. Nothing
is more precious than to spend time with those we love. From time
to time we should review what's really important in our lives and
rethink how we spend our time. It's what life is all about—meaningful
relationships.

Solomon observed the importance of friendships (Ecclesiastes
4:9-12). Paul recognized the importance of marriage (Ephesians
5:21-25). God created people to be in relationship with Him and
in relationships with one another. Friends who work on a task can
rejoice together in its accomplishment. Spouses rejoice in their children. Friends can help each other—if one should fall, the other is
there to help her up. Those who have both a strong relationship with
God and strong friendships with other believers will have bonds that
strengthen life's joys and limit life's sorrows. Friendships among believers are precious, for they have the bond of Christ and of eternity. We
should both *find* good friends and *be* good friends.

Ask yourself this one question: *In light of eternity, how am I spending my time?*

*Dear Lord, help me to make the most of my time, even
when I cannot control it. In Jesus' name I pray. Amen.*

Struggling with Why

*We also rejoice in our sufferings, because we know
that suffering produces perseverance; perseverance,
character; and character, hope. And hope does not disappoint us, because God has poured out his love into our
hearts by the Holy Spirit, whom he has given us.*

ROMANS 5:3-5

Loss, divorce, death, cancer…ever ask God why? I think we all
have. But to "rejoice in our sufferings"? If making sense of pain in our
lives is not difficult enough, now we're also told to rejoice in it? You're
probably wondering what Paul was thinking when he wrote this. *Was
he in his right mind?*

He sure was. He saw the purpose of pain—to build perseverance
and character. But it only comes when we're obedient to God in the
midst of the *why.*

You may never receive the answers to the *why* questions you have.
Even with Job, God neither explained his suffering nor helped him
make sense of his loss (see Job 1–2). In the end, Job found peace, not
in answers, but in a deeper desire to live in the presence of God (Job
42). Your love for Him in return cannot be based on how you think
He is treating you. Instead, you are to trust Him and His goodness
regardless of what happens to you or how you feel—simply because
He is God.

*When trials and problems come my way, Lord, and all
I want to do is ask why, forgive me. Calm me with Your
presence. Soothe me with Your love. Show me that by
enduring I will become stronger and closer to You. Amen.*

About Forgiveness

Father, forgive them, for they do not
know not what they are doing.
LUKE 23:34

Becky can't sleep at night. She keeps having nightmares about her mother, who abused her as a child. Even though her mother has been dead for ten years, Becky still struggles to forgive.

Why would God even ask Becky to forgive someone who caused her so much pain?

Giving forgiveness is difficult. It involves letting go of the past and moving on. It almost seems as if we are letting the other person off the hook, without any punishment or responsibility to make restitution. Where is the sense in that?

It begins with realizing that God in His mercy forgave you. We are all sinners who have been forgiven by God. Not only the sins you have committed but also every sin that you will ever commit has been paid for with the blood of Jesus. He forgave the sins of all mankind through His death on the cross.

Once you understand that you have been forgiven, you are released to unload the burden of pain in your past. A clearer understanding of Christ's gift of forgiveness will develop by forgiving those who have hurt you.

Abuse is the most difficult type of pain to forgive. Unburden yourself. Cling to Christ, who is your strength. Do not allow the sin of the abuser to continue abusing you! Forgive because God is there waiting to renew your strength and help you move on, refreshed and ready to celebrate your life in Him!

Dear Lord, thank You for forgiving me. Help me learn to forgive
as You forgave. Help me release my burden of pain. Amen.

An Abundance of Gifts

There are different kinds of gifts, but the same Spirit.

1 Corinthians 12:4

Teaching, counseling, shepherding, showing mercy, giving...as Christians, we have each received different gifts from God. You may know what your gifts are. It's just obvious to you. You may be comfortable speaking in front of a crowd, leading a Bible study group in your church, or counseling others. Or maybe you make cooking supper every night look as easy as Rachael Ray.

On the other hand, you may have no idea what your gifts are. Let me help!

The Bible tells us that we all have *different* gifts. It doesn't say that to some significant gifts are given and to others, insignificant ones. All gifts are given equally by God. God doesn't rate our gifts—that's a human thing we do. "All these [gifts] are the work of one and the same Spirit, and he gives them to each one, just as he determines" (1 Corinthians 12:11).

You are gifted! Perhaps you have the gift of patience (carpooling the soccer team three times in one week without screaming); love (driving your teenage daughter to the mall *again*); listening, patience, and love (a phone call with your mother); thoughtfulness (sending an e-mail to your pastor showing appreciation); or caring (mailing a sympathy card).

God's dream for you is that you would use the gifts and abilities He has perfectly designed for you! God has gifted you abundantly. Look for His gifts. Cherish them. Use them to bring glory to Him.

*Dear Lord, help me use the gifts You have given me
to honor You. Give me confidence to seek and find the
talents I have and share them with others. Amen.*

Crazy About You

Dear friends, let us continue to love one another,
for love comes from God. Anyone who loves is a
child of God and knows God. But anyone who does
not love does not know God, for God is love.

1 JOHN 4:7-8 NLT

God is crazy about you. You are His child, His princess. He showers you with every good thing. Instead of obsessing over what you *don't* have, think about all you *do* have: His love and attention, fresh air, and clean water. Food, shelter, and a place of belonging. Health, family, friends...I am sure you can keep going from here.

Once you are aware of how lavishly God loves you, pass that love on. Everybody needs at least one person in her life to be crazy about her. And God has no greater plan than to use His people to share His love and grace. Whom can you show that love to—a friend, Mom, Dad? Maybe its an aging relative or your kids. Sure, some parents will do it, but others don't seem to care. They just get by. Kids deserve better, and God wants you to be a parent who's crazy about her kids. Your children are God's children too and are worthy of His love—and yours!

God sometimes places people in our lives who need our love and attention. And He loves to let others know of His great love for His people through you. Can you see them?

Look around you. Let God use you to be the one who is crazy about somebody else in the world.

Dear Lord, thank You for being a God of lavish love. Let me rejoice
in the love You give me every minute of every day. Let Your love
explode in my heart and cascade into the lives of others. Amen.

Doing What's Right

So let's not get tired of doing what is good. At just the right
time we will reap a harvest of blessing if we don't give up.

GALATIANS 6:9 NLT

Sometimes life is not fair. We keep doing good, we take care of our kids, we volunteer our time for a church committee. We pay our bills on time. Overall, we do a pretty good job of living. But nobody really notices, and we certainly don't get any major rewards for it. Meanwhile, movie stars can misbehave, go through rehab several times, act immature or just plain stupid, and get away with all of it. It's enough to want to give up and say, "Why am I trying so hard?"

Don't give up. Don't get tired of doing good. If we hang in there and continue on the path of life God has shown for us, there is a reward—we will reap a harvest of blessing. This is a pretty significant quantity guaranteed here. It's not just one or two blessings, or even a few; it's an entire *harvest* of blessings.

God's dream for you is fulfilled as you follow the pathway of right living—the path of righteousness. It's the way of life He has dreamed for you. Don't get tired of walking with the Lord—the path of life is pleasant, and the rewards are huge.

Dear God, take away any discouragement and confusion
I have about which path to follow in my life. Let me
clearly see that the path of righteousness makes dreams
come true and leads to a harvest of blessings. Amen.

Each Day a New Beginning

God gives wisdom, knowledge, and hap-
piness to those who please him.
Ecclesiastes 2:26 GNT

A fresh start—a new beginning every day—that's what you have with God. An opportunity to live your life as a pleasing testimony to Him, to be a light to the world, to live in a way that shows you serve a living Savior who continues to renew you each morning. He forgives your sins, wipes the slate clean, and forgets all about what you've done in the past. Now that's something to be happy about!

God reigns! Regardless of what lies ahead, God is always in control. Throughout the centuries He has showered His people with His goodness and mercy in spite of all the adventures and misadventures humans have endured. Our God is an awesome God. He is powerful and almighty! Believe it! Believe Him right now!

Since the beginning of time, we humans have sinned. But God has been there to forgive us seventy times seven (Matthew 18:21-22 NKJV). And God continues to love you no matter what. He loves you when you mess up and have to try again. He loves you just the way you are now. He loves you while you try to change and become more like Him. Wherever you are, His love surrounds you.

Now go live for Him!

O God and Father, thank You for giving me a new beginning
each day. Let me rejoice each morning in Your love and
bountiful blessings. Fill me with the excitement that I have a
new chance of shining Your light and love on others. Amen.

Fear Not!

Fear not, for I am with you; be not dismayed, for I am
your God. I will strengthen you, yes, I will help you,
I will uphold you with My righteous right hand.

ISAIAH 41:10 NKJV

When I was a little girl, my bedroom was on the other side of the house from my parents'. The doors to the cellar and the garage opened close to my room. I was scared to death to go to sleep at night.

Fear is a powerful emotion. It can immobilize us, make us physically ill, sap our energy, and make us weak. Even Adam admitted to God, "I heard you in the garden, and I was afraid because I was naked; so I hid" (Genesis 3:10). Of course, he had something to hide!

Since that time, God has been reassuring people not to be afraid, because our nature consists of fear. In His desire to be in relationship with us, He loves us and is "for us." More than 100 times the phrase *Fear not* or *Do not be afraid* is used in the Bible by God, an angel of the Lord, or leaders speaking to and reassuring the people.

God promised His people over and over again that they had nothing to fear because He was with them. That promise is true for you too! You don't have to be afraid of anything—neither death, nor life, nor angels or demons, nor the present or the future, nor any powers in all of creation, because nothing can ever separate us from God's love (Romans 8:38-39).

And God's love is perfect. "There is no fear in love. But perfect love drives out fear" (1 John 4:18). God's dream for you is to embrace His love for you.

Dear Lord, drive out the fear in my life and replace
it with Your perfect love and peace. Amen.

God Is Greater than Anything

My dear children, let's not just talk about love; let's prac-
tice real love. This is the only way we'll know we're living
truly, living in God's reality. It's also the way to shut
down debilitating self-criticism, even when there is some-
thing to it. For God is greater than our worried hearts
and knows more about us than we do ourselves.

1 John 3:18-20 msg

How well do you know yourself? Many of us are still searching to
know what we want in life, what we want to do, what makes us happy,
what makes us unique from every other individual on earth. It's a little
scary to think God knows more about us than we do. Yikes!

There is true comfort in knowing the Lord knows us so well.
Think about it. He has known you since you were conceived and
being formed in your mother's womb (Psalm 139:13-16). This is God's
reality—knowing and loving you!

I hate my thighs...I hate my hair...I hate my big feet...I'm fat and
*ugly...*whatever your thought may be, change it now! You are pleasing
to Him. You are the great love of His life. You matter. Every part of
you has been created by the Lord of lords and the King of kings. You
are beautiful to Him and are a cherished child of the Almighty.

If you need to know yourself better, know this: You are a child
of the King, and He loves you. He has crowned you with glory and
honor (Psalm 8:5), and He has prepared a place for you in His kingdom (John 14:2).

O God of all love, help me to see myself through Your eyes. Help
me to realize that You love me beyond anything I can imagine and
that You made me and know me as I am. Stifle my urge to be self-
critical, and let me learn to live in Your favor and love. Amen.

A Dwelling Place

*My people will live in peaceful dwelling places, in
secure homes, in undisturbed places of rest.*
ISAIAH 32:18

Have you ever thanked God for the gift of place? God has graciously placed you where you are—in this country, this city, this place, this time. God has given many of us a tremendous gift. Because of where He has placed us, we can live and worship in freedom, use our talents, and safely walk out in the street to shop, attend church, visit friends, or go to school.

On the other hand, for millions of people, the gift of place looks very different. They are not free to come and go as they like or to live up to their greatest potential. Every day the news is filled with stories of unrest and uprisings, terrorist attacks and assassinations, violence and poverty. The Middle East, Africa, and parts of Asia are all experiencing unrest. Even in the United States, many live on streets of instability. People who have known only unrest and scarcity hear about a world of peace and prosperity and think it's nothing but a dream.

If you've been blessed with a peaceful dwelling place, even though it may seem wild and crazy at times, take time to thank God today for where He has put you. And pray for those less fortunate. If you live in a place of chaos and instability, I pray God would show you favor, that He would protect you from any physical danger, and that He would provide the resources for stability within your home and peace within your heart.

*Dear Lord, thank You for placing me where I live. Be with those
who are less fortunate, especially those living in poverty and violence.
Protect them and provide for all of us a dwelling place of peace. Amen.*

Handling Change

I the LORD do not change.
MALACHI 3:6

Change is powerful and strange. We lose sleep over it. We fight it. We stand firmly against it. We worry about it. And sometimes we crave it! Yet so much of it is out of our control.

Change comes wrapped in a lot of different packages. Your daughter announces her engagement. Your spouse announces he's found a job opportunity 700 miles from home. Your church decides to try a different style of worship. Your doctor's news leaves you in shock.

Change is also inevitable. But you can be assured that you will be able to face whatever change comes your way. Our security is not in the state of the economy, the status of a job, or the strength of the structure we live in. Our security and strength lie in God, our Creator. The all-powerful, all-controlling One promised in writing that He never changes. You have His word on it!

Knowing that God doesn't change, that He is our strong foundation, doesn't mean you won't have a few anxious moments or sleepless nights. You will still be overwhelmed the first morning after a move when nobody can find the toilet paper. But ultimately you know that although the world may be changing around you, either by your choosing or not, your God stands firm. Your God does not change!

His love will always be with you whatever change you experience. Find comfort in His strength and His peace, today and forever!

Dear Lord, thank You for being unchanging! Help me find confidence, assurance, and peace in this fact so that regardless of what happens in my life, I know I can count on You! Amen.

He Enables Me

So Paul and Barnabas spent considerable time there, speak-
ing boldly for the Lord, who confirmed the message of his
grace by enabling them to do miraculous signs and wonders.

ACTS 14:3

Enabling has been given a bad rap. It implies a weakness or inability
to handle things on our own. But to be enabled by God is completely
different. We may think we are strong and capable, but we will always
need God's enabling.

As a daughter of the King, you do not stand alone. You do not
have to be strong in all things. His dream for you includes cooperating
with Him in everything you do. He wants to enable you to do what
He has called you to do. Only through His power can you fulfill His
purpose and see His dream come true. Jesus said that apart from Him,
we cannot bear fruit (John 15:4). But you belong to Him, and through
His power and His grace you are enabled to accomplish all things.

Just as God enabled Paul and Barnabas to perform miracles and
wonders, He enables you in every way to perform and accomplish
everything from your daily routine tasks to the challenges you perceive
as impossible. When all you want to do is yell to God, *But I can't do
it*...add one more word to that plea: *alone.* God does not expect you
to do what He has called you to do all by yourself.

You *can* do it! Just don't try it on your own. Turn that plea into a
prayer. God will hear you.

O Lord, I can't do it alone. Enable me to face the tasks You set
before me and to accomplish what needs to be done. Let me feel Your
strength, Your comfort, Your support throughout my day. Amen.

Impossible Dreams

With man this is impossible, but not with
God; all things are possible with God.
MARK 10:27

Some people take New Year's resolutions quite seriously. Others take them casually. Most have stopped bothering. The best-kept resolutions usually involve things we can control, like these:

I'll lose ten pounds.

I'll walk every day.

I'll spend more time in prayer.

I won't get angry.

I'll have a regular devotional time.

I'll stick to a budget.

I won't use my credit cards.

I'll love my husband more.

Have you ever thought about doing something really big? Something really impossible?

Think of something that you dream about but that you feel utterly incapable of doing. Now, place that impossibility before God. Talk to Him in prayer about it *every day.* Ask Him to handle this for you. Listen to see if He guides you into taking action. Then take a step!

Pray for what you think is impossible and expect a miracle. God's dream is for you to attempt the impossible—for His glory!

O God, in my weakness I think almost everything is impossible
for me to handle. Help me to trust You with all these
things, to lay them at Your feet and believe that with You,
everything is possible. I pray this in Christ's name. Amen.

The Waiting Game

*I wait for the LORD, my soul waits, and
in his word I put my hope.*

PSALM 130:5

Sometimes God's dream for us seems to take forever to unfold. When our plan doesn't seem to be pulling together the way and in the time we would like, we sometimes think that God has forgotten all about His plan. We may even consider the possibility that perhaps His dream was literally just that—a dream, and not something that was meant to become a reality.

Don't lose hope! It's time to look back on the stories of the Bible concerning people who were promised great and marvelous plans but then waited for what seemed like a lifetime to see them fulfilled.

Sarah and Abraham were promised a son. But years passed, they grew old, and still they did not have the promised baby. Finally, at the age of 90, Sarah had a son (see Genesis 17:15–18:33; 21:1-6). Can you imagine raising an infant at 90 years old?

The Israelites waited 400 years in Egypt to be freed from slavery. Then their dream of living in a land flowing with milk and honey was postponed an additional 40 years! But they eventually settled in the land God had promised them.

God's dream doesn't always happen overnight—it sometimes takes a lifetime. But He promises it will come true. Don't run ahead. Put your trust in Him. Great things come to those who wait!

*When my plans don't work as I had hoped, Lord, don't let
me get discouraged. Fill me with hope that Your dream for
my life is yet to unfold, just as You promised. Amen.*

Lessons for Living God's Dream

For the grace of God has appeared,
bringing salvation for all people, training us to renounce
ungodliness and worldly passions, and to live self-
controlled, upright, and godly lives in the present age.
TITUS 2:11-12 ESV

Living out God's dream for your life can seem a daunting task. You may feel weak and alone, and experiencing all God has for you may seem totally impossible. Perhaps you're almost ready to give up before you've begun. If that's the case, consider that you may be trusting in your own strength and ability.

You can live God's dream and be the woman He wants you to be through His grace—not your own power. His grace teaches you to shun the things of this world and to have self-control. His power strengthens you when you are weak. His love shines through you onto your children, your family, and your friends. His mercy keeps you humble.

God's dream is bigger and more magnificent than anything you can imagine. But this dream will unfold for you only if you walk close to the Lord. Open your heart to Him, listen to His Word each day— read it, study it—and stay in close communication with Him through prayer. Yield your heart to Him. Don't go on your own power, go on His! You *can* live out His dream for you!

Dear Lord, surround me with Your love and grace so I can live
for You. Teach me to rely on You for the strength to overcome
evil, love constantly, and rest securely. May every aspect of my
life be a realization of the dream You have for me. Amen.

Little Dreams Everywhere

The LORD has done great things for us, and we are filled with joy.
PSALM 126:3

Many of us think that God's dream for us will be fulfilled in miraculous, one-of-a-kind experiences. But stop and think for just a minute. Perhaps God's dream for you is revealed little bits at a time, unfolding quietly throughout each minute of every day.

A baby's cry. The warmth of the sun. Snow that sparkles on a winter morning. The sound of your daughter's laughter. A hug from your son. The voice of a friend. All of these and many, many more are God's little dreams coming true each hour, each day of your life.

Don't overlook these things. They are precious little gifts given freely and generously by our Father. Consider these gifts as little dreams floating down from heaven.

Each day, train yourself to be more aware of little dreams coming true. Open your eyes and mind to magical moments and quiet blessings. Start writing them down on a scrap of paper or in a special journal. Soon you will see your life from a different perspective and start seeing that perhaps much of God's dream for you is right before your eyes.

It's here. Right now! It's all around you. Look closely—don't miss it!

Open my eyes, Lord, to see that Your dream for me is being fulfilled in little moments and happy experiences every day. Let me appreciate them and cherish them as gifts from You. Amen.

Finding a Wheat Field

*If you listen to these commands of the LORD your God that
I am giving you today, and if you carefully obey them…
you will always be on top and never at the bottom.*

DEUTERONOMY 28:13

Close your eyes. Picture yourself walking through a wheat field in the middle of the countryside. No cars, no phones, no computers, no distractions. Drink in the warm sun, the gentle breeze, and the sweet smell of honeysuckle nearby. Open your arms and feel the freedom of God's grace.

Discovering God's dream for your life is about experiencing God—His grace, His mercy, and His freedom. Do you approach each day with a spirit of expectation? A belief that God is in the midst of everything you do?

Those who live at the top do. They see the blessings nobody else does. They rarely miss a sunset. They feel the embrace of a child's hand and love to enjoy a good belly laugh. They experience God and are thankful to Him for the little everyday things.

Don't take life so seriously all of the time. The glass is half full! Go for a walk today. Take in the beauty around you. See a comical movie. Stop and smell the roses. Find your wheat field and be free—in Him.

*Dear Lord, help me stay close to You so I can hear Your
voice and follow Your commands for my life. Help me
to focus on more of You and less of me. Amen.*

Living in Gentleness

Let your gentleness be evident to all.

PHILIPPIANS 4:5

In our fast-paced world, where we seem to always be in a hurry, gentleness is a fruit of the Spirit that we often overlook.

In Galatians 5:23, gentleness is listed right next to self-control. That's a pretty obvious grouping. They seem to go together. You certainly can't have gentleness without some self-control. We are also instructed to clothe ourselves with gentleness and patience to achieve holy living (Colossians 3:12).

When was the last time you thought of yourself as being gentle? Perhaps it was recently as you cradled and soothed a crying infant, or you gently administered a Band-Aid to a scraped knee or pressed a cool washcloth to a fevered forehead. But were you gentle when correcting your child or speaking to your spouse? So often we forget about being gentle in *all* aspects of our lives.

Christ referred to Himself as gentle when He said, "Come to me, all you who are weary and burdened, and I will give you rest. Take my yoke upon you and learn from me, for I am gentle and humble in heart, and you will find rest for your souls" (Matthew 12:28-29). What a wonderful invitation!

Gentleness requires that you banish harshness from your speech and actions. It comes from a peaceful heart and a quiet spirit, from asking Christ to dwell within so you will emulate His characteristics. As you become gentle, peace will become a part of your life and home.

O Lord, let me be gentle in every aspect of my life so I will bring quiet and calm to my little corner of the world. Fill me with Your gentle Spirit so my calm and self-controlled life will show Your love to others. Amen.

Making Plans

Those who plan what is good find love and faithfulness.

PROVERBS 14:22

Planning is a good thing. It gives direction and meaning to your day—your life. God has a plan for everything and everyone. He has been working out His dream plan for the world since the beginning of creation. He also has set a great example for you to follow.

Some folks think planning is a bother, but I believe that if you really want to make things happen, you need a plan. Carving out a time for making family memories can require some major planning. Deciding to go back to college requires a plan. You can transition careers and explore new options smoothly with a bit of planning. If you don't work at it, little events and obligations will clutter days, weeks will fly by in a blur, and you won't be any closer to your dream than before.

This is when you start to realize that if you don't have a plan, it just won't happen! Planning is necessary to make your dreams come true. Little by little, day by day, if you move in the direction of the dream, you will get closer to it. As you work on each step, pray and share each detail with the Lord. He will guide your thinking, and your path will unfold according to His will. You need to do your part in seeking out His plan and working toward its fulfillment.

Work with God, make a plan, and make it happen!

O Lord, I know You are the ultimate planner. Help me to take the necessary steps to see Your dream for my life come true. Nudge me, Lord, to take the first step in the right direction. Amen.

On Track with God

*So if you find life difficult because you're doing what
God said, take it in stride. Trust Him. He knows
what He's doing, and He'll keep on doing it.*

1 PETER 4:19 MSG

When life gets difficult (and it does from time to time), you may begin to wonder, *Whatever happened to the dream God had in mind for me? Everything I see has turned into a nightmare.* That's an ordinary reaction, but nothing has happened to the dream. God is still with you and still has a plan. If you're doing in life what you know God wants you to do, life will include difficult seasons, but you can take them in stride.

God never said that once you believe in Him and follow Him, your life would be free of trouble. In fact, Jesus told everyone when He was here on earth, "In this world you will have trouble. But take heart! I have overcome the world" (John 16:33). You will encounter problems, but He will help you through them.

If you're feeling that God is far away, that trouble is overcoming you, it's time to take a closer look at your life. Are you walking with the Lord? Are you doing what He has asked you to do? Or are you running from what you know you should be doing?

Take inventory and readjust your life. Get back on track with God and trust Him.

*O Lord, help me to examine my life and be sure I'm doing
what You want me to be doing. Make me confident that I am
going in the right direction—Your direction. And if I'm on the
wrong path, Lord, please make me bold to make the necessary
choices and changes to get back on track with You. Amen.*

Powerful Words

*Words kill, words give life; they're either
poison or fruit—you choose.*

PROVERBS 18:21 MSG

How often have you opened your mouth, said something, and then realized your mistake and had to apologize profusely?

All of us make mistakes. We open our mouths and speak before we even think about what we say. Ouch! That can get us into big trouble and lead to all kinds of misunderstandings and hurt feelings. Too late we realize we said something stupid or revealed way too much. Both thoughtless comments and intentional verbal jabs can be like poison. The snide remark over someone's appearance. The catty comment intended to be a putdown. The shared secret that you promised not to repeat. Those words are deadly as poison.

If you are careful and think about what you say, your words can be enriching and bring life to others. With God's help you can learn to be more mature, think carefully, and speak more thoughtfully. Careless talk and insensitivity can only cause problems. Guarded minds and prayerful remarks will be blessings to others. Words to your children, your spouse, or your friends can be soothing, build self-esteem, quiet anxiety, or shower them with joy. Or they can be pure poison that kills the relationship and hurts their spirit.

Watch your words. They can be the poison that kills or the fruit that yields sweetness and satisfaction. The choice is up to you!

*Dear Lord, fill my mind and heart with love and peace and purity
so that what pours out of my mouth will reflect those thoughts.
Help me to guard my tongue and always be slow to speak. Amen.*

Kindhearted Women

A kindhearted woman gains respect.
PROVERBS 11:16

All of us are eager to know God's dream for our lives. But have you ever thought that you might be part of the fulfillment of God's dream for someone else? God uses His people to fulfill His plans. You can brighten someone's life with an act of kindness. A Japanese proverb says, "One kind word can warm three winter months." That's what we all need—any time of year.

Start with a kind word. Then move into a kind action. Even the smallest act of kindness can bring sunshine to another person's life. It can change the world into a brighter place for a moment—maybe for a lifetime.

Here are some ideas to get you going:

- Invite a friend over for tea in the afternoon.
- Compliment the checkout clerk at the grocery store.
- Call someone you haven't been in touch with for months.
- Tell your pastor he's doing a wonderful job.
- Send a thank-you note.
- Offer to babysit for your neighbor.

Think about it. If each person in the world shared just one positive word or one small action of kindness, our world would be a much better place!

As pastor E.V. Hill said, "When God blesses you, He rarely has you in mind."

*Fill me with your loving kindness, Lord, so that
I can show kindness to others. Amen.*

A Cheery, Prayerful, Thankful Kind of Gal

*Be cheerful no matter what; pray all the time; thank
God no matter what happens. This is the way God
wants you who belong to Christ Jesus to live.*

1 Thessalonians 5:17-18 msg

If you're looking for a verse to use as your motto for living, this is it. Be cheerful, pray, and be thankful—always! Not just some of the time, but *all* of the time. Wouldn't our lives be more joyful, more exhilarating if we put into practice the three parts of this verse?

"Be cheerful no matter what." Sounds a bit over the top, but what a delightful way to live this would be. It would be even greater to be around a bunch of people who actually believe and do it! As Christians, we have no reason to be gloomy. Our calling and the life God has for us are far more glorious than what is happening on earth. And Christ has secured that future for us.

"Pray all the time." Various translations use different words to describe being in prayer with the Lord all the time: endlessly, never stop, without ceasing, continually. So never stop praying. Do it all the time. Your life should be one prayer fest to God—praising Him, thanking Him, and asking for His assurance, guidance, peace, and wisdom.

"Thank God no matter what happens." If you truly believe that God can work all things together for your good (Romans 8:28) and that nothing can separate you from His love (Romans 8:39), then you can do this. He loves you and wants only the best for you, showering you with all kinds of gifts. Be thankful always!

*O Lord God, may my life be a constant prayer of praise
and thanksgiving to You. Let my heart and my thoughts
be in constant communication with You. Amen.*

Pure Perfection

*Create in me a pure heart, O God, and
renew a steadfast spirit within me.*

PSALM 51:10

When you think about being God's princess, what jumps into your mind? Being good? Purity? Perfection? All of that is true. As His royal princess, you should reflect His purity, His light, His glory. But sometimes we feel as if we are far from the perfect princesses we desire to be.

Maybe this vision seems completely illusive to you—just a distant dream. You have a good reason for feeling that way. Sin runs rampant in the world, and you are impure because of your sinful nature, which began in the Garden of Eden. But the existence of sin doesn't have to keep your dreams from coming true. God sent His Son to undo what Adam and Eve did. He came to conquer sin, and He won! The great Victor has given you the victory over sin!

As God's child, you get to live out the dream He has for you. You have the opportunity to become all you envision a royal princess of the King of kings to be. You are precious and pure in His sight because you are washed in the Savior's blood. All you need to do is ask, "Wash me, and I will be whiter than snow" (Psalm 51:7).

*Dear Lord, You have given me the victory over sin. Let
me live as Your child, perfect and pure. Purify my heart
and make my spirit stand firm for You. Amen.*

Rejoice and Be Glad!

This is the day the LORD has made; let
us rejoice and be glad in it!
PSALM 118:24

Knowing how God wants you to live out His dream for you is pretty simple: joyfully and one day at a time. I've talked to a lot of women over the years at various conventions and speaking engagements, and I am always surprised that this simple truth seems to escape so many. I often hear women say something like this: "I am burdened with guilt and baggage from my past and scared to death about the future."

This seems to reveal a disconnect with some basic but wonderful news about believing in Christ Jesus as your Lord and Savior. He has taken away the guilt and shame of your past life. Your past sin and burdens are all gone. You are now a new creation. You are free!

As for the future, God has clearly spoken about not worrying because that won't change a thing. "Do not worry about your life… Who of you by worrying can add a single hour to his life?" (Matthew 6:25,27).

Knowing that God has forgotten the past and has the future under control, all you are left with is the present. You only have to deal with today. Today is a gift, yours to enjoy to the fullest. Ask Him for forgiveness, and then forgive yourself. Now, move on!

Rejoice and be glad! This is God's day. This is God's moment. Find happiness in it and be happy!

Dear Lord, forgive me for fretting about a past and a future that
I cannot control. Let me rest in the knowledge that You care about
me, that You have everything carefully planned for my life. Give me
peace to face each new day with a joyful and happy heart. Amen.

Role Models of Humility

Humble yourselves before the Lord, and he will lift you up.
JAMES 4:10

I have a challenge for you. Think of someone you know who you would consider to be a humble person. Here's an even harder challenge: Think of five people.

Could you do it? Humility is not the way of Hollywood, Wall Street, Washington, or the rest of the world for that matter. Humility is the way of Christ and is part of the dream God has in mind for us. Throughout Scripture we are taught about the virtues of humility:

- "When pride comes, then comes disgrace, but with humility comes wisdom" (Proverbs 11:2).
- "Humility and the fear of the LORD bring wealth and honor and life" (Proverbs 22:4).
- "Before his downfall a man's heart is proud, but humility comes before honor" (Proverbs 18:12).

The Utmost Humility Award of all time goes to Christ the Lord, who "humbled himself and became obedient to death—even death on a cross" (Philippians 2:8). He is the example you are to follow for knowing how to be genuinely humble. By reading about and closely examining His life and His actions, you will know how to be humble with others and with God.

"The way up is down." I've heard it so much that I sometimes forget how true it is. As a Christian, you carry the name of Christ. In His name you can be the role model of humility for your children and everyone you meet!

O Lord, teach me Your way of humility. Let my life exemplify Your obedience and humility here on earth. Amen.

Seeking Help from Others

Two are better than one, because they have
a good return for their work.
ECCLESIASTES 4:9

Part of God's plan for being in relationship with others is that we stop striving to do everything by ourselves. So many times we choose to play the martyr and take on a project or an event. We refuse the help of others, thinking it's easier to handle it all on our own. Or we're too proud to ask for assistance, thinking it's a sign of weakness or lack of skill. But including others to handle the work is a good idea.

Moses, the great leader of the Israelites, was called by God in a burning bush and told to do miraculous things in order to free the people from the iron grasp of Pharaoh. But even he could not do all God needed him to do on his own.

"Carry each other's burdens, and in this way you will fulfill the law of Christ" (Galatians 6:2). Burdens, joys, sorrows, projects, accomplishments—sharing these things is part of God's plan for all of us.

Are you playing the martyr, trying to handle everything all by yourself?

Stop! Don't do it alone! Ask lovingly for assistance. Accept offers of help graciously. And afterward, offer thanks to everyone. Doing it together will be good for you, good for the body of Christ, and pleasing to the Lord.

Dear Lord, show me the way to graciously accept help from others.
Diminish my prideful spirit of being able to handle everything by
myself. Give me wisdom when I'm asking for help or offering assistance
so that I truly share my burdens and tasks with others. Amen.

Sing for Joy

*Come let us sing for joy to the LORD; let us shout aloud
to the Rock of our salvation. Let us come before him with
thanksgiving and extol him with music and song.*

PSALM 95:1-2

Every day is worth singing for joy. But wait...*every* day? Even *this* day?

Some days don't seem especially joyful. We all have days that we would rather never repeat again. We make a major mistake at work. A child is sick. Something is making a weird noise under the hood of the car. Our husband is crabby. No money in the checkbook. No milk in the refrigerator. All those things can steal our joy.

But the kind of joy that is easily lost and gained again when the sun shines and the paycheck is deposited, when our husband is perky and the kids are in perfect health, is not the kind of joy that the Bible talks about. The kind of joy that causes us to shout to the Lord with thanksgiving, to dance before Him, is a deeper joy that nothing in this life can steal away from us.

This joy is the joy of the Lord! The joy that comes from knowing He is the Rock of our salvation. Through Him we are washed clean from our sins and free from our past. Through Him we have the promise and the hope of eternal life and eternal joy that knows no limits. That is a joy worth singing about. That is a joy that makes every day a day for singing to the Lord!

*Let my life be filled with the joy of Your salvation, Lord.
When my life is empty of joy due to the problems of the
world, remind me, Lord, of the great joy that only You can
give. Fill me with the joy of Your salvation. Amen.*

Strength from the Lord

I lift up my eyes to the hills—where does my help come from?
My help comes from the LORD, the Maker of heaven and earth.

PSALM 121:1-2

It's comforting to know that we serve a God who is stronger than anything in the universe. Hills and mountains may symbolize strength to many of us, but our God is more powerful, more constant than any mountain. He is stronger than the highest mountain peak, mightier than any mountain range, more majestic than the "purple mountain majesties."

So what does this mean for you?

You may be weak, but He is always strong (2 Corinthians 12:9).
His strength sustains you (Psalm 29:11).
God is always in control (Psalm 21:1).

So what do you need God's strength to do?

Do you face a health crisis that is leaving you anxious?
Do you face changes to your lifestyle that leave you insecure?
Do you have a financial crisis that leaves you panicking?
Do you face a broken marriage?
Do you struggle with a rebellious teen?

God's dream for you is to look up to the hills or to the sky and to ask Him for help. He will give you renewed strength and hope. He wants to help you through everything you face.

O Lord, I'm calling for You to help me. I need Your
strength to face the burdens in my heart. Be with me,
Lord. Take my hand. Give me hope. Amen.

The Great Communicator

*For everything that was written in the past was writ-
ten to teach us, so that through endurance and the
encouragement of the Scriptures we might have hope.*

ROMANS 15:4

Our God is not only a God of relationship; He is a God of communication. What a wonderful God we serve! He has given us His voice
and His words. From the early days of Moses, God's word has been
preserved and passed down from generation to generation.

Even today we have these words, written out in our very own
language, that we can read and understand for ourselves. We do not
need interpreters or high priests to tells us what God is saying. He
speaks to you and me each day through the Bible if we take the time
to read it and listen to Him. We have the privilege of reading these
words over and over, studying them, filling our hearts with them, and
letting them come to life in our own words and deeds.

And God does not leave us guessing as to who He is or where to
find Him. We do not have to guess how He wants us to act or live our
lives. It is all very clearly given in words of love and truth through the
Bible. How can we keep our ways pure? By living according to God's
Word (Psalm 119:9).

God's dream for you is to hide His Word in your heart so that you
do not stray from His commands. Open the Word today and listen
to what He has to say.

*Thank You, Lord, for communicating with me. I especially
praise You for providing Your Word in my language so I can
come to know You better through reading and studying. Let
me feel Your presence and open my heart to You. Amen.*

The Life God Envisions

So flee youthful passions and pursue righteousness, faith, love, and
peace, along with those who call on the Lord from a pure heart.
2 TIMOTHY 2:22 ESV

Notice what the apostle Paul tells Timothy about how we are to
live our lives:

Righteousness is right living. Doing and thinking the right things.
Obeying the laws of the community you live in. Abiding by the rules
of society. Being mature and responsible for your thoughts and actions.
"Blessed are they who maintain justice, who constantly do what is
right" (Psalm 106:3).

Faith as the Bible defines it is "being sure of what we hope for and
certain of what we do not see" (Hebrews 11:1). It is that innermost feeling
of trust in God regardless of the circumstances you find yourself in.

Love. Love of self, love of others, love of God. All three are important to fulfill God's dream for your life. The Bible gives you a beautiful
summary: "Above all, love each other deeply, because love covers over
a multitude of sins" (1 Peter 4:8).

Peace in your life begins with peace in your heart. As you have a
peaceful heart, you will have a peaceful home. Your peaceful home
will create a peaceful community. And your peaceful community will
create a peaceful nation. "There is deceit in the hearts of those who
plot evil, but joy for those who promote peace" (Proverbs 12:20).

Go after this way of living. Share it with other Christians. A life
filled with righteousness, faith, love, and peace is the life God dreams
for you.

Father, help me to yield to the life You want for
me—to shun youthful passions and seek the path of
righteousness, faith, love, and peace. Amen.

The Power of God

God's voice thunders in marvelous ways: he does great things beyond our understanding. He says to the snow, "Fall on the earth," and to the rain shower, "Be a mighty downpour."

Job 37:5-6

Ice storms, blizzards, hurricanes, tornadoes, wildfires…when God's power displays itself in nature, man's plans are halted. Schools are cancelled (the kids love that). Roads are closed. Activities are postponed. Airplanes are grounded. Even the people who are the most determined to get somewhere are hindered by acts of nature.

We easily forget that God is in control of nature—and everything else! All of man's striving, busyness, and eagerness to get somewhere, to negotiate a contract, to finalize a major project, to make money, or to build and accomplish can be stopped in an instant by rain or wind or fire.

Major storms can be God's way of saying, "Stop. Slow down. Reprioritize your life. Remember that I'm in control."

You can strive for bigger and better things all the time, but it is by His hand and by His gracious goodness that you get up in the morning and do what He has called you to do. Just as you can't create a snowstorm, you can't fulfill God's plan for your life on your own terms. You can struggle and hurry and fret about many things, but God is in control, and He will accomplish His will in His timing, in His plan.

So relax in the Lord's presence. He is in control. All things will be fulfilled in His perfect timing.

All-powerful God, help me to realize that Your ultimate plans cannot be hindered in any way. Let me relax in knowing You are always in control—even of the fire and the wind, the rain and the snow. Amen.

Walking in the Light

*When Jesus spoke again to the people, he said, "I am
the light of the world. Whoever follows me will never
walk in darkness, but will have the light of life."*
JOHN 8:12

You were made for the light. In the beginning of everything, before
the world began, darkness covered everything. And then God called
out, "Let there be light," and He separated the light from the darkness
(Genesis 1:3-4). On the fourth day He created the sun, moon, and
stars to give light on the earth. After all this light filled the universe,
He created humans. You were created in the light.

Perhaps this is why many are afraid of the dark, why we sometimes
dread the long, gloomy days and the dark of winter. We were created to
live in the light and walk in the light. Sin, however, entered this world
and darkened some of the pure light. But with Christ's coming—the
light of world—light has overcome the darkness.

Through some of the darkest years of Judah's history, the prophet
Isaiah spread hope and promise with his words. "The people walking in darkness have seen a great light; on those living in the land of
the shadow of death a light has dawned" (Isaiah 9:2). They lived in
hope of this coming promise for hundreds of years before the Messiah
came. We are blessed to be on the other side of this prophecy—we
know He came!

Jesus, the light of the world, came to shed His light and His love
on every aspect of life. Walk with Him. Walk in the light!

*Dear Lord, help me to see Your light wherever there is
darkness in the world. Let Your light shine in and through
me. Let me walk always in Your light. Amen.*

Pouring Out Your Soul

I am a woman who is deeply troubled…
I was pouring out my soul to the LORD.
1 SAMUEL 1:15

Hannah, the mother of the great prophet Samuel, was distraught. The Scripture says that her womb was barren. She couldn't have children, and that ate at her like a cancer. She wept bitterly. It made her crazy, so much so that Eli described her as a drunken woman. She cried to God.

I bring your attention to Hannah's life for an important reason. Emotional pain from issues like infertility goes deep into our soul. Nearly one in six couples struggle with infertility. And people often misunderstand or are unaware of the wounds in our hearts. God never is. He is there. He listens. And He gives strength for the journey. Whether or not He opens our wombs is always in His plan. But He will always heal our wounds and see us through.

Whatever the result, we should commit or dedicate our future and even our children to the Lord for His service.

Lord, You know the troubles of my heart. May it no longer be barren. Make it fertile, alive, and passionate for You. Amen.

What a Friend

Friends come and friends go, but a true
friend sticks by you like family.
PROVERBS 18:24 MSG

What a friend we have in Jesus,
all our sins and griefs to bear,
what a privilege to carry
everything to God in prayer.

I love that song. It is wonderful to be reminded what a great friend Jesus is. Being in communication with Him through prayer and sharing everything with Him are tremendous privleges. The relationship we have with Jesus is a model for what our friendships here on earth should be like.

Just as you share all your problems and concerns with Jesus, you should share them with true friends. Friends will listen. Friends will care that you are hurting. Friends will rejoice when you are happy and cry when you are sad.

First John 1:7 says, "If we walk in the light, as He is in the light, we have fellowship with one another, and the blood of Jesus, His Son, purifies us from all sin." When you risk becoming vulnerable with true friends, you can walk together in the light. You can hold each other accountable and make certain not to give the devil a foothold (Ephesians 4:27). So go ahead and pick up the phone. Go for coffee. Send an e-mail. Write a letter or a special greeting card. Be certain to show a friend that you care today.

Dear Lord Jesus, thank You for being my friend. Thank
You for the friends You have provided for me. Help me look
to You for the ultimate model of friendship. Amen.

Which Way to Go?

Thomas said to him, "Lord, we don't know where
you are going, so how can we know the way?"
JOHN 14:5

We've all had one of those dreams where we're late for something—an appointment, a final exam, a plane—and we're rushing around but can't find the necessary paperwork, the correct building, the specific room, or the right gate. Everything is shrouded in fog or a vague blurriness that keeps us from achieving our objective.

Thank goodness that knowing the way to God is not like that at all. It's clearly revealed in Scripture. There's no guessing game with God. His Son clearly stated, "I am the way and the truth and the life. No one comes to the Father except through me" (John 14:6).

The way of life for us comes through Jesus as we look into His face, reach for His hand, follow Him, and surrender to Him. This is the way of life that is full of richness and love here on earth, and it's the way of eternal life with the King of kings and Lord of lords.

Look up into the wonderful face of Jesus and know that He is all you need to live both here on earth and forever in heaven.

The way is clear. He is the way. Follow Him!

Show me the way, Lord, so I can live the life You have
planned for me to the fullest. Let me stay focused on
You and follow where You lead me. Amen.

Leaving a Legacy

*I have been reminded of your sincere faith, which first
lived in your grandmother Lois and in your mother
Eunice and, I am persuaded, now lives in you also.*

2 TIMOTHY 1:5

"Well done, good and faithful servant!" (Matthew 25:21). These are the words that I desire to hear from God when I enter heaven. To be found faithful is a life goal I have set for myself, and I hope to pass on that legacy to my children.

What do you want others to say about you when you are gone? What kind of legacy do you want to leave behind? I want to be like Lois and Eunice. Paul described them as having "sincere faith" that they passed down throughout the generations of their family.

Decisions you make today contribute to the legacy you are leaving behind. Leaving a legacy worth remembering requires staying close to God the Father and abiding in Him. Become a student of His Word and continue faithfully in your prayer life. Remain pure and holy as He is holy. Guard your heart and mind against sin. Our life itself is short, but our life legacy lasts for eternity! What you do in this life will echo forever!

*Dear Lord, help me remain faithful today. Help me to build
a lasting legacy that is worth being remembered, a legacy that
directs those who come after me to follow You. Amen.*

Other Great Harvest House Devotionals for Women

EXTRAORDINARY WOMEN
Julie Clinton, president of Extraordinary Women ministries, shares biblical illustrations, life examples, and prayers throughout this book. You will learn to embrace extraordinary living when you discover God's dream for you, make every day count in surprising ways, and release control to take hold of God's freedom.

10-MINUTE TIME OUTS FOR BUSY WOMEN
Grace Fox encourages you to make time for what matters most—your relationship with God. Her real-life stories and Scripture-based prayers will help you understand God's truth and apply it to everyday life.

ONE MINUTE WITH GOD FOR WOMEN
Hope Lyda, author of the popular One-Minute Prayers series, shares inspiration and spiritual nourishment in devotions created for a woman's busy life. Along with Scriptures and prayers, this gathering of meditations provides the gifts of wonder and faith, deeper relationship with God, encouragement for tough stuff, and reminders of mercy and grace.

GOD'S BEST FOR MY LIFE
We all need fresh grace each day, says Dr. Lloyd John Ogilvie. This devotional by the former pastor of Hollywood Presbyterian Church and chaplain of the United States Senate offers 365 days of insight and encouragement.

THE DAILY BIBLE® DEVOTIONAL
F. LaGard Smith, creator of the bestselling *Daily Bible,* leads you on a devotional journey through the Bible. Verses in chronological order serve as the inspiration for 365 original messages that go beyond the narrative transitions of the *Daily Bible* to illuminate practical truths, faith foundations, and biblical promises.

HARVEST HOUSE
PUBLISHERS

To learn more about books by Harvest House Publishers
or to read sample chapters, log on to our website:

www.harvesthousepublishers.com

HARVEST HOUSE PUBLISHERS

EUGENE, OREGON